Praise for *A Land of Hard Edges*

While U.S. migrant policy limps on bleeding feet and ignores its own hungers, a million uprooted poor huddle along our southwestern border. Ready or not, these mostly Mexican migrants join other American migrations—slaves escaping the plantations, Irish leaving a potato famine, Jews fleeing Nazis, and Okies driven out of the Dust Bowl. Retired nurse Peg Bowden joined with border angels to help, and she brings us personal stories and photos of migrants and volunteers one hopeful face at a time. Instead of proverbial loaves and fishes, now it's grandmothers handing out burritos and hot coffee. Come spend a day with Bowden in the soup kitchen called *el comedor*. Filled with courage and compassion, this uplifting book is the best on the human side of the immigration equation that I've yet read.

—Bill Broyles, writer, educator
author of *Sunshot: Peril and Wonder in the Gran Desierto*

Peg is one of the most compassionate people I know, and I've known her for 37 years since we started teaching nursing in Ashland, Oregon. Peg's experiences on the border not only reflect her dedication to helping others, but lend themselves to her thoughtful and analytic approach to social issues. *A Land of Hard Edges* provides a very insightful yet informative approach to understanding the issues around immigration.

—Rosalie Caffrey, Ph.D. Professor Emeritus
Oregon Health & Sciences University

Peg Bowden, RN, found her retirement to the Arizona/Mexican border surprisingly disrupted by Border Patrol vehicles, helicopters and lost migrants. She chose to respond by immersing herself in the compassionate efforts of the Samaritans, capturing and presenting vividly her observations of the tragic and hopeful stories of all affected. Her on-the-ground involvement and graphic descriptions of the experiences give real life to this story. Christian R. Amoroso, MD

continued . . .

W0006779

In this compelling memoir of her experiences feeding and clothing migrant men, women, and children in Nogales, Sonora, Peg Bowden takes readers behind metal fences and wire barriers to view the human consequences of U.S./Mexico border policy. The stories she tells are often gut-wrenching, but she gives us hope in a world of angry political rhetoric in the resilience of the human spirit and the healing power of good works.

—Bruce J. Dinges, Ph.D., editor of *The Journal of Arizona History*

Peg Bowden breathes life into crucial border issues so often lost in polemic. She sits us down to lunch with desperate, destitute Mexicans, our neighbors. And with warmth and wit, she shows us how humanity transcends lines on a map.

—Mort Rosenblum, reporter, author, educator

In a world divided by borders and marked by the violence and suffering that these same divisions create, Peg Bowden's book stands as an eloquent testimony to the power of acts of love toward the other: the alien, the destitute, and the 'illegal' migrant. Driven by a sense of compassion toward the immigrants she attends to in the *comedor* on the U.S./Mexican border, Bowden documents the everyday lives of both the extraordinary volunteers and the resilient immigrants who cross her path. This is a book that articulates a profoundly urgent vision of care, healing and love in the face of a world riven by border politics. Acutely reflexive, at once poetic and political, this compelling book asks the reader to reflect on the transformative power of humanitarian activism as a way of challenging the violent status quo of contemporary border politics.

—Dr. Joseph Pugliese,
Associate Professor Research Director of the Department of Media,
Music, Communication and Cultural Studies,
Macquarie University, Sydney, Australia,
Author of *State Violence and the Execution of Law*

A LAND OF HARD EDGES

A LAND OF HARD EDGES

SERVING THE FRONT LINES OF THE BORDER

Peg Bowden

PEER PUBLISHING

A LAND OF HARD EDGES

Copyright © 2014

Peer Publishing
For more information about this book and its author, visit pegbowden1942@gmail.com
1505 W. St. Mary's Road, #379, Tucson, Arizona, 85745

Edition ISBN 978-0-9892009-9-8

Cover design by Pete Garceau
Interior design by Catherine Leonardo

Author's note: This is a work of nonfiction. Some names of the people in this book have been changed to protect the privacy of the individuals.

This edition was prepared for printing by The Editorial Department
7650 E. Broadway, #308, Tucson, Arizona 85710
www.editorialdepartment.com

Printed in the United States of America.

For Lester, Cheyenne and Sage

"For I was hungry and you gave me food, I was thirsty and you gave me drink, I was a stranger and you welcomed me."

Matthew 25:35

"When your family has been killed, there is no place to cry."

César, a migrant from Guatemala, September, 2012

Table of Contents

Foreword

PAUL THEROUX

Sometimes the strangest things happen near home; and these can be the most enlightening and transformative. People go to Africa or Asia and return shocked or surprised by what they've seen—remarking on the poor, the dispossessed, the hopeless, the luckless, the victims of a pitiless system. But you don't have to travel far to observe highly colored exoticism, or dramatic difference, or extreme injustice, or even to witness the plight of the poor or dispossessed. That is one of the messages of Peg Bowden's marvelous book. Another is that there is hope.

There are two towns called Nogales, divided by an international border, and emphasized by a big fence. A simple painted sign on a wooden board—"To Mexico"—is propped near the door in that fence. This enormous barrier is monumental, a multimillion-dollar symbol in steel that depicts our national obsession with threat and contagion.

In a lifetime of crossing borders I find this border fence the oddest frontier I have ever seen. The frivolity of it is the price our country is paying for its delusions. When I beheld it, looming forty feet over me as I stood on a main street in Arizona beside my parked car, I looked for an entryway. And of course there it was, just where Morley Avenue ended—past J.C. Penney's and Kory's Clothing—a turnstile that gave Arizona access to Mexico, just ten steps from one country to the other, a door in the wall, the foreign country at the end of a hot sunlit street.

The wall—representing our frontier—is made of enormous two-story high steel rectangles that had been recycled from plates that had served as a runway in the desert for Operation Desert Storm. Welded together these plates run as far as the eye can see along the perimeter of this part of Arizona, the big rusty bulwark of a fenced-off republic. (I first saw it in 2012. It has since been made higher and stronger and impenetrable.)

I walked through the narrow door—no line, no other formalities—into the state of Sonora, in the *Estados Unidos Mexicanos*. I was instantly, unmistakably in a foreign land, on bumpier roads, among vaguely distressed buildings and some boarded-up shop fronts, and the mingled aromas of bakeries and taco stands and risen dust.

I was lucky in having Peg Bowden with me that day to guide me. Peg, a retired nurse, brought me to the *comedor*, a shelter run by American Jesuits near the Mariposa gate just about a mile from downtown Nogales. She told me that she worked there a few days a week, crossing the border from Arizona. I wondered what had motivated her. She said she was so shocked by the attack by an armed man on Gabrielle Giffords in Tucson in January 2011 that she decided to do something humane. "I needed to connect with something positive." She joined a group of Samaritans—"a bunch of renegade senior citizens whose mission is to prevent deaths in the desert"—and she volunteered at the *comedor*.

As a trained nurse she was useful, treating bullet wounds and severe hypothermia and the effects of starvation and exposure—common among border-crossers. She told me, "Last week we had a girl who'd been lost in the desert for three days. She was fourteen."

Iniciativa Kino para la Frontera, the organization that directs the activities of the *comedor* ("dining room"), was named for Father Eusebio Kino, a Jesuit astronomer and cartographer who came to Sonora in the mid-1600s. This set of buildings, and a dormitory, near the Mariposa border crossing at the western edge of Nogales was started in 2009 by a group of Arizona Jesuit priests, among them Father Peter Neeley

"I don't have a parish," Father Neeley told me. He was pastor at the *comedor*. "Symbolically this is a parish. The Jesuit mission is live with or work with the poor."

He called it a soup kitchen but it was more than that. It was a soft landing for migrants—some long-termers, some border jumpers—who had been thrown out of the U.S. Broke, many of them ill and all of them hungry, they were given meals, two weeks' accommodation, help with clothes and medicine, a little money, and a bus ticket home. None of it was government-funded; it was underwritten by churches, donations and grants

"Migrant smuggling used to be a mom-and-pop business," Father Neeley said. "Say a hundred dollars to get to Phoenix. But now it's more like two thousand dollars." But trafficking in migrants has changed. The cartels were now involved. "People are more profitable than drugs and less trouble. With human smuggling there's less jail time."

The fence loomed here as it did in the middle of town, but this was another revelation. A hundred and sixty lost souls, most of them adults, though there were four small children, were eating breakfast the day I visited. One was a woman eight months pregnant with a four-year-old in tow, from Veracruz, picked up while walking across the desert, running away from "a desperate family situation." Another woman: "I wanted to see my sister in L.A. They caught me in the desert."

But some had spent many years in the U.S. Maria, an older woman, told me, "I spent twenty years in Napa picking strawberries. My husband and children are there. I came to Mexico for my father's funeral. And now I can't go back." Nor did she have a home in Mexico anymore.

They were soft-spoken, humbled, half-starved and desperate. A woman in her twenties, Rosalba, had spent four days in the desert. She had blistered feet, a deep wound from a cactus thorn and severe infection. Her wish was to go to Anaheim, to work.

Alejandro had lived in Charlotte, North Carolina, for thirteen years, mainly working in a Chinese restaurant. "They were good people. They were immigrants too." But he was stopped for a minor traffic violation, had no papers to show, and arrested. Arnulfo had a similar story—eleven years in the U.S., first in New York and later Nebraska, working as a carpenter. He was pulled over for speeding and ("no papers") detained without trial for four months, and put onto the bus.

The saddest case to me was a woman from Oaxaca. Abandoned, with no money, no prospects, and no hope of making a living in Oaxaca, she left her three children in the care of her mother, and crossed the border with four other

A moment of grace at *el comedor.*

women, in the hope of finding work. Somehow separated from the other women she was found in the desert. Her eyes filled with tears when she talked about her children.

"It's Sophie's Choice," Peg Bowden said.

She accepted her fate, and I will never forget the sight of her alone at the table, a plate of food before her, eyes tightly shut, hands together uplifted in prayer.

Introduction

There are moments in our lives that change us forever. They move us emotionally. Sometimes they move us to action. We've all had them: the Kennedy assassination, the Martin Luther King assassination, the walk on the moon, the morning of 9/11—the horrific day the twin towers of the World Trade Center fell into a cloud of dust and rubble.

On January 8, 2011, in a Safeway grocery parking lot in an upscale neighborhood of Tucson, Arizona, a madman created unspeakable havoc, shooting nineteen people in broad daylight. Six died. One of them was a small child.

It was the Tucson Massacre.

On that sunny January day, I was standing in line at a movie theater in Green Valley, Arizona, to see *True Grit*, the remake of the classic old-time western movie. The sun was beating down, and my husband and I impatiently waited for the theater doors to open. A man next to me was fiddling with his cell phone messages and suddenly said to everyone within earshot, "Oh my God! Gabby

Walking the wall.

Giffords has been shot, and a bunch of others are dead along with her!"

"Naw. You gotta be kidding. Is this some sort of weird joke? Gabby? Shot?!"

Immediately I felt nauseated and dizzy, as if I had been kicked in the stomach. I did not want to go into the movie and watch more shoot-'em-up images and gunslinging heroes. This must be some kind of hoax.

For the next weeks, the country pondered the meaning of this heinous act of violence. Gabrielle Giffords, U.S. Democratic representative from Arizona, was out and about shaking hands with constituents. On this cloudless January day, the kind of day that makes shopping for groceries and greeting a member of Congress a pleasure, Giffords was critically injured with a bullet to her brain. As of this writing, her recovery has been nothing short of a miracle, but this act of insane brutality changed many lives irrevocably. Mine was one.

The Tucson Massacre jolted me out of my retirement mode. I was living with my husband on a ranch south of Tucson near the Mexican border. Life had slowed down to a comfortable trot: I painted, hiked, and played timpani in a local band. Pondering what this tragedy meant, I decided to get more involved in the issues of my community. I felt an urgency about doing something but wasn't sure what to do.

Immigration and the numbers of migrants crossing the desert close to my home were at the forefront of my consciousness. In fact, they were in my face each time I drove to town. I watched silently as Border Patrol agents thrust lines of young Latino men into their vehicles. Little by little I ventured into the world of border politics and the humanitarian crisis I saw unfolding a few short miles from my home.

I decided to become involved in a small migrant aid station and soup kitchen across the border in Nogales, Mexico. Joining a group called the Green Valley Samaritans, I gradually learned about the complexities of immigration.

I woke up.

This is a story of the front lines, specifically a place known as *el comedor*, which in Spanish means "the dining area." I am a volunteer at the *comedor*. It is a humble enterprise on the Mexican side of the border and is the stage for some of the most dramatic and profound work done on the other side of the wall. The *comedor* is a place of refuge for migrants traveling north from Mexico and for those who have been deported from the United States. Feeding a hearty breakfast and dinner to more than one hundred migrants a day, the shelter is a binational project of the Kino Border Initiative (KBI), an adjunct of the Jesuit Refugee Service.

How I came to be involved with this small outpost is one of those peculiar turns that can take on lives of their own. This is the story of my year of awakening as a volunteer at *el comedor.*

I have occasionally changed the names of both migrants and aid workers in this book. Every story is true, however, and the themes are things that matter to me. I apologize if I have left out some detail, or perceived a situation or person differently from my colleagues and friends at *el comedor.*

CHAPTER ONE

A Land Of Hard Edges

It's December in Ashland, Oregon. I'm pulling myself together on this frigid morning getting ready for work, watching the ice fog settle in for the day. It creeps along the street in front of my house like some giant meandering caterpillar.

I dream of sitting on a sunny rock in the mountains of Arizona and gazing at the horizon a hundred miles away. Having grown up in Tucson, my soul still speaks to the prickly pear cactus and mesquite of the Sonoran Desert. After thirty years as a nurse in Oregon, I'm fantasizing yet again about retirement where the sun is a daily fact of life. Especially on this murky morning. I daydream about hiking the Grand Canyon and sleeping out under the stars.

Arizona is a land of hard edges. The rocks are sharp and jagged, and my hands and knees are often bruised when I clamber over them. Everything you touch has a prickly sharpness—the cactus, the mesquite trees, the creosote bushes. There is an occasional scorpion under the

Samaritans assist injured migrant at the *comedor*.

bathroom rug; sometimes a rattlesnake creeps into the shade of the patio for a nap. When a stinging fire ant finds a spot under my sandal strap, I writhe in pain for hours. The desert is amazingly beautiful, stark, forbidding, inviting, inspirational, blazing hot and icy cold. Mere words fall short. There is nowhere on earth quite like it.

The lush green forests of Oregon are idyllic, and the ground is pliable. The edges of rocks are soft with moss. My feet sink into the earth. You can't see much of the sky. The ponderosa pines offer a canopy of green, and the stars disappear from view.

I like to walk on terrain that is solid, rugged and

unyielding. Bring on the relentless heat of Arizona summers. Bring on the craggy cliffs and hard edges of steep, bouldered canyons. I'm through with the December drizzle of Oregon winters.

Sooner than expected I retired from a career in public health nursing after a serious brush with ovarian cancer and abruptly decided to move back to Arizona and live out my desert vision. Basically I am a desert girl. I like to scale rocks, find a flat spot to sit and watch sunsets.

So it was with a sense of relief and longing that I resolved to return to the desert and the smell of a simmering pot of pinto beans on the stove. I missed the desert and the colors and flavors of the Southwest. I missed the heat. I missed a decent meal at a Mexican restaurant. I needed a rest. I was ready to retire and hang up my stethoscope.

My life has not often gone as planned. There have been marriages and divorces. There have been serious illnesses, and the finances have waxed and waned. Living as a single mother often felt like all work and no play. But through it all two delightful children have shown me what love is all about. We survived the rough times.

My husband and I married back in the 1970s, divorced after ten years and then remarried twenty-five years later.

"Ten years on and twenty-five years off," he is fond of saying.

Our children are still stunned by the arc of this love story.

With the progeny now grown and launched, we decided to move back to Arizona, choosing a spot near the Mexican border in the San Cayetano Mountains. We wanted to live together after a long and varied history both as a family and apart. We decided to come home. To the desert.

It is easy to lose oneself in this wild place. We live fifteen miles from the nearest town. Driving out the gate of our ranch is often a trip that neither of us wants to make. Better to isolate oneself from the troubling news of the outside world. We pick up our mail twice a week from a mailbox ten miles away. We do not subscribe to a daily newspaper. Reading *The New York Times* on my computer, the local news is not on my radar. After all, I'm retired now.

I must confess that I was nervous about living close to the border on a remote and isolated piece of desert wilderness. The evening newscasts and the media in general were full of stories about the "illegals," and national broadcasts warned of drug smugglers and bandits roaming the countryside.

Living in the borderlands is like living in a third nation, with one foot in Mexico and one foot in the United States. Things are different here. The freeway mileage signs are calibrated in kilometers. The grocery store in the nearest town, Rio Rico, features a dozen varieties of *chile* peppers, Mexican cheeses and corn husks for *tamales*. Most of the people are bilingual, speaking both Spanish and English. Radio stations feature Mexican music and the staccato cadence of people speaking Spanish. Lines of trucks packed with tomatoes from Mexico speed toward Tucson and points north on the one major freeway.

There is an immigration checkpoint located approximately twenty-five miles from the Mexican border on Interstate 19, the major freeway heading north to Tucson. All vehicles must stop so federal agents can determine the citizenship of the occupants. You are asked if you are a citizen of the United States, and sometimes where you were born. Officers in uniform peer through the windows looking for anything suspicious—illicit cargo such as drugs, weapons or people stuffed in the trunk. Cars and trucks line up, and a well-trained dog sniffs the tires and trunks of the waiting vehicles for contraband. If there is any suspicion of drugs or human smuggling, there is a flurry of activity and the vehicle is pulled aside for a thorough inspection.

Once when I was hauling one of my timpani in the back of my Jeep, the officer opened the trunk and tapped curiously on the copper bowl of the kettle drum. I play the drums in a local concert band and was rushing to a rehearsal.

"So what the heck is this?" he asked, bemused and curious. And bored.

He had never seen a kettle drum before and asked me several questions about the nature of this strange cargo. Maybe he thought this was a great hiding place to stash a kilo of marijuana. Maybe he just wanted to have a friendly conversation. When I explained that I am a musician and was in a hurry for a dress rehearsal, he allowed me to pass through the checkpoint.

I am both impatient and resigned to these intrusions on my commute to Tucson. The militarization of the border is a fact, and I've learned to live with it.

Life in Arizona has changed since my youthful years in Tucson in the 1950s. As a young girl, I crossed into Nogales, Mexico, frequently with my family for shopping sprees with relatives from Iowa, and festive dinners in some of the elegant restaurants along the street.

Back then the border crossing into Mexico was a rickety gate dangling on a squeaky, rusted hinge. A decrepit two-strand barbed-wire fence designated the border and disappeared after a block or two. Often I didn't bother walking through the gate but just slid under the fence. Customs officials on both sides were casual, friendly and welcoming. No passports or identification were necessary.

As a child I was puzzled about borders and boundaries. The American side of Nogales looked about the same as the Mexican side. Well, maybe there were a few differences. The Mexican side was more colorful, more vibrant, more fun.

"So where is the black line on the ground, like on the maps?" I asked my mother. How a dilapidated wire gate could divide one country from another was beyond my comprehension.

But by the 1990s and the first decade of the new millennium, thousands of people from Mexico and other Latin American countries were migrating north, and the politics of immigration had become big news throughout the country. A huge forbidding wall separated the two Nogaleses, and armed guards patrolled the port of entry.

The last thing on my mind was getting involved in local affairs and controversy, but the drama of people on the move was happening in my neighborhood. Migrants crossing without the proper papers were getting picked up every day in the desert, and Border Patrol vehicles were seen regularly close to our home.

I was reluctant to face these situations that I saw unfolding regularly on my repeated drives to town. Feeling safe behind the gate of our ranch, I found it easy to ignore the troubled times on the border. I could avoid reading about the violence in Mexico. But I could not erase the image of a massive migration of people from my mind.

WAKING UP

The faces haunted me.

Driving the desert roadways in southern Arizona, I often would see rows of young men sitting alongside the highway grabbing a bit of shade under a mesquite tree. Their eyes were cast down, dark hoodies covered their heads, and plastic jugs of water sat beside them. Sometimes I would slow down and try to get a better look at their exhausted, defeated faces.

I looked at them; they looked back at me. Who are these people? Drug smugglers? Terrorists? Why are they sitting there? Where do they go from here?

Streaked with the dust of the Sonoran Desert, they looked to be teenagers or perhaps in their early twenties. Border Patrol agents, eyes shielded behind their Ray-Bans, walked back and forth in front of the sad little group. The agents looked as glum and forlorn as their captives. The year was 2002, and my husband and I had recently moved to the desert.

A couple of times I gave a half-wave as I drove by. Smiling and nodding, a few young Latino men waved back. One held up two fingers giving me the peace sign.

"Hey, do you need any extra bottles of water?" I asked a Border Patrol agent on an especially hot day in June.

"We've got enough. Keep on moving," the agent told me. He waved me on. End of discussion.

I wish I could have seen the eyes shielded behind those sunglasses. Driving away from the group by the roadside, I wondered what the Border Patrol agent was thinking about my offer of water. More to the point, I wondered what he thought of his captives, who looked hot and thirsty sitting in the roadside gravel in the sun.

Initially I thought the migrant groups must be drug smugglers caught with their cargo of marijuana or cocaine. That's what was often emblazoned in the headlines of local newspapers. The media were full of accounts of the "illegal aliens" from Mexico. They were dangerous, they left maimed, decapitated bodies in the desert, and because of them there was a shroud of evil blanketing the border states. My out-of-state friends cautioned me to be careful, as they thought I lived in a war zone fraught with frequent gunfire and mayhem.

This went on for years. I told myself to mind my own business. Homeland Security knows what it's doing.

But somehow the image of the migrant Latinos at the side of the road stuck with me. They didn't look like villainous drug dealers but instead looked like sixteen-year-olds lost in a strange land. I began to feel like a privileged white woman living on the rich side of a gated community whenever I passed them by. Speeding toward town, I would glance in the rearview mirror and notice how their eyes followed my car.

Once my husband, Lester, and I went camping in a remote area close to the Mexican border. We encountered an American biologist collecting insects and plants. The field scientist mentioned that there might be "travelers" coming through at night but that they were friendly and quiet and we should not be alarmed. He had been camping out for a week collecting his specimens. He seemed relaxed and comfortable with the nighttime trekkers.

Later as Lester and I bedded down on a tarp and looked

at the stars, I was a bit nervous and excited about the prospect of migrant travelers quietly coming through our campsite. We both slept soundly and didn't hear or see a thing. My dreams that night were of lines of people walking through the desert singing soft Mexican ballads.

At times when I drove to town, I watched as the Border Patrol agents packed their captives into green and white trucks that looked like dogcatcher vehicles. Driving past these scenes by the side of the road did not feel right. I needed to pay attention to something that was happening in my neighborhood, but I didn't know how to do it. When I ignored the plight of the young men by the side of the road, I tried to look the other way. Intimidated by the uniforms, the weaponry and the presence of the military personnel, I attempted to go about the activities of daily life on my trips to town.

My thoughts ran uncontrolled as I watched these roundups of Latinos. It reminded me of the roundups of other minorities in our history—the Japanese Americans during World War II, the African Americans during the civil rights movement, the Native Americans during our relocation schemes on the reservations. Always people of color.

I thought, too, about the Germans during the Nazi regime, as they passed by the military officers loading Jews into boxcars. People drove by, business as usual. They looked the other way.

My impotence and inability to confront what I was witnessing troubled me deeply. I couldn't just drop it. The images kept me awake. The faces continued to haunt me.

And still I did nothing.

THE SAMARITANS

Quite by accident I picked up a book that talked about the work of a group called the Green Valley Samaritans. I began to attend its bimonthly meetings in the small town of Sahuarita, Arizona. I loved this group immediately.

The Samaritans are a loosely organized, very committed group of mostly retirees who meet every other Monday at the Good Shepherd United Church of Christ in Sahuarita. There were one hundred people gathered in a circle at my first Samaritan meeting, most of them white-haired and pushing seventy or older. Beginning with a few moments of silence, the group quietly contemplated the numbers of migrants in the desert trying to reach a safe place to live and survive. The designated leader closed the silent meditation with the words *"Vaya con Dios."* Go with God.

During the meeting, many took notes. They were all on time—my kind of people. There were several reports from various interest areas: the desert search group, the water drop group, the *comedor* (kitchen/shelter) group, the *basura* (trash) group. It was clear that the Samaritans didn't sit around and talk endlessly about what should be done. They jumped into their cars and did it.

I'm not a group person and don't do well discussing strategic goals and volunteering for committees. What I loved about the Samaritans was their activism. The group was not tied to rigid structures, rituals, egos and endless meetings. The Samaritan mission was clear and direct: to prevent deaths in the desert. Discussion and reports revolved around the numbers of migrant deaths in the neighboring desert and the needs of deported migrants in Nogales,

Mexico, at the *comedor*. There was an urgency here that appealed to me. The work felt vital and important.

Never mind the politics of it all. Never mind all the legal claptrap about entering the United States without documentation. I am neither a lawyer nor a politician, and I will leave these questions to others. If people are dying in the desert, you give them water and food and whatever else they may need to survive.

This is what a civilized society does. You pay attention to those young men in hoodie sweatshirts being rounded up by the side of the road. This sounds like the America where I grew up.

There are more than one hundred Green Valley Samaritans actively involved in pushing for social change on the border. Many quietly and courageously respond to what they see around their homes and neighborhoods. We hear reports of groups of migrants walking through Arizona golf courses and residential areas trying to figure out how to get to Tucson. Samaritans approach anyone in need and do what they can to help.

The Samaritans are full of retirees whose activism is both inspirational and provocative. Immigration issues are complex, and sometimes we step over each other in our eagerness to help. To do something. Giving out needed clothes, shoes, food and medical supplies seems like a pittance— like a band-aid on a festering wound. But at least the Samaritans are in the desert providing water and aid if needed, and at the *comedor* bearing witness to thousands of migrants. Assisting with life-saving support seems like a logical first step.

The chief mover and shaker of the Green Valley

Samaritans is Shura Wallin, a fiery woman from Berkeley, California, who moved to Arizona in 2000. She saw the numbers of deaths in the surrounding desert and decided to do something about it.

Shura is a free-flowing, upbeat person. She is all heart and reaches out to the least among us. Walking to the *comedor* each week with Shura is a real meet-'n'-greet experience. Weighing probably ninety pounds, Shura walks with a rapid, determined gait. I am in a trot to keep up with her. She is obsessed with the injustice of poverty and reaches out to the poor with unabashed tenderness and concern. Plus, she is just plain gutsy and will milk any situation for a laugh at her own expense. I don't think Shura has ever been embarrassed in her life.

And so began my entry into the world of humanitarian activism.

FIRST TIMES

I decided to commit to volunteering weekly at the *comedor.* Here at this border aid station, Samaritans assist migrants in several ways.

The Samaritans volunteer each Tuesday, helping with breakfast and bringing needed clothing and medical supplies. If migrants speak of their plans to cross north into the United States without proper papers, Samaritans counsel about the increased military presence in the desert, the dangers of extreme weather conditions, the long distances to towns or cities. Pointing out a map posted at the *comedor,* we show the numbers of deaths each year in the Sonoran

Desert. We strongly advise migrating Latinos to reconsider their plans and return to their homes in Mexico and Central America.

For those who have recently been deported from the United States, Samaritans will sometimes buy bus tickets to their home villages farther south.

My goal was to do this for one year and learn as much as I could about migration and the policies of the United States toward immigration.

I jumped into this arena of humanitarian service in January 2011, making my first trip south to the *comedor* on a midwinter's day. It was just a few weeks after the Gabrielle Giffords shooting and I was nervous about venturing across the border. First times leave an indelible impression. I remember this initial trip to the humble shelter well.

—⁄⁄⁄⁄—

The day is crisp, cold and sunny. I am accompanied by five other Samaritans. We each carry supplies in our backpacks for the small first-aid station, as well as shoes and clothing for distribution.

The walk itself is a lesson in America's answer to immigration. The first image of border life is the wall—the biggest, tallest, most gargantuan wall in North America. The United States is building this wall, and it is massive. Twenty feet high at various points. Like no other wall in this hemisphere. The message is clear: Stay out. You are not welcome here. We don't want you in our version of America.

On the U.S. side of the border, burly men in uniform carry assault weapons and many pounds of military hardware. These are the men and women of Immigration and Customs Enforcement (ICE), U.S. marshals and Border Patrol agents. They walk around the border checkpoint as we pass by. I say hello to a few of them and they do not answer. Their gaze is focused somewhere over my head. They are all business.

The air is rank with dust and dirt from the huge tractors and excavating machines scooping out the earth to make way for continued work on the wall that separates the United States from Mexico. Our group is directed several times to a dirt path that is not clearly marked as we dodge the builders and their machines.

The whole experience is oddly exciting. The noise and shouting of the workers as they shovel tons of earth is impressive and unnerving. There are cars and trucks going and coming through the port of entry. The lines are long. Trained dogs sniff at the vehicles and their handlers respond to the canine signals. I think about the deep financial recession of 2011 in the United States and witness the billions of dollars being spent on a wall.

We pass through the rotating iron gate and are in Mexico. The mood changes immediately. You know you are in a foreign country as soon as you pass through that gate. Walking by the Mexican immigration officials, we are greeted with *"Buenos días,"* and there are smiles all around. We use the bathrooms on the Mexican side of this border checkpoint, which they graciously make available to us. We still have at least a half-mile to go before reaching *el comedor*. The mean age of the members of my Samaritan group is probably 70. Bathrooms are a priority on this chilly morning, especially a toilet that flushes.

A long line of truckers and cars is backed up on the Mexican side, three rows deep, probably a half-mile or more. Peddlers and newspaper hawkers are busy working the scene. There are balloons, candy treats, pottery, *tamales* and religious charms for sale. Truckers and tourists give us a thumbs-up, and Mexican music from the car radios fills the air. An ice cream man from Honduras offers us coconut ice cream on this cold winter morning.

"Maybe later," we tell him. Several of the vendors rush over to greet Shura, our designated leader today. She seems to know everyone and calls every other young man her "son." There are hugs and greetings as I see her slipping half of the men dollar bills with instructions to "Be careful" and "Give this to your kids." The mood is festive. A man calls out, "You are all angels!" It is a bit of a circus.

A big overhead sign greets us with *"Bienvenidos a Nogales."* Welcome to Nogales! I'm pretty sure I'm going to like this trip, and we haven't even gotten to the *comedor* yet.

Looking across the busy highway as we hike along, I see a long line of people in front of a scooped-out indentation in a hillside. Blue tarps and cyclone fencing enclose the little cave-like structure. This is the *comedor*, the aid station that serves hundreds of meals each day. There is a queue of people waiting outside quietly, many shivering on this cold morning in January. Several women are wrapped in blankets for warmth. The men huddle in thin T-shirts waiting for the shelter to open for breakfast and the possibility of a warm jacket. The soft cadence of Spanish is everywhere.

I see a woman limping, her face strained with pain. A couple of stray dogs hover around an overflowing trash can looking for scraps of food.

A young woman holds a sleeping baby swaddled in a shawl amid the jostling of people waiting to enter the *comedor.*

It takes me a moment to realize that these people are migrants recently deported from the United States. Some have traveled up from Central America and southern Mexico and are preparing to cross the border in search of a better life. Many have been in detention centers (lockup prisons for migrants) in the United States and were just released into Mexico. Their dreams have been stalled.

The people from Honduras and El Salvador cannot believe how cold it is on this morning. The indigenous peoples from villages in southern Mexico are stunned when they see how tall the wall is. They learn how many armed police and Border Patrol agents will look for them if they decide to cross into the United States. Most have no idea how far the walk is to Tucson, where they hope a ride awaits. Their *coyote* guides—people who lead people across the desert for a price—tell them two days; we tell them seven days if they are lucky.

One person tells me he is on his way to New York and restaurant work. Another is off to Kansas City and a roofing job. Their sense of distance and direction is hopeless. Their eyes shine with hope and determination. They live for *el sueño americano,* the American dream.

Looking over the roomful of young men and women as they wait for a nourishing breakfast, the migrants look like working-class people—the landscapers, the restaurant workers, the hotel maids, the nannies, the fast-food service providers. Some are farmers from central Mexico, their hands callused, their bodies bent. Many have held steady jobs in the United States and for various reasons have been deported and separated from their families. They look stunned, numb and quietly grateful for this safe place of refuge.

IN THE BEGINNING

The *comedor* didn't just happen. At first, several Mexican families living near the Mariposa port of entry into Nogales, Sonora, noticed that hundreds of people were being dropped off daily in the streets near their homes. Often these disheveled travelers had been bused across the line into Mexico by United States Border Patrol and ICE agents and left to wander at two or three o'clock in the morning.

The year was 2007, and eight Mexican families witnessing this parade of misery met to discuss the crisis. The pilgrims were lost, disoriented and had no money or food. Most were Mexican citizens. Their clothes were rags, and their shoes were often without soles. The local families could no longer passively watch the lines of hungry, injured immigrants passing through their neighborhoods and do nothing. By way of response, they decided that each house would commit to making one hundred burritos a month, or eight hundred total.

Standing under a bridge on a Mexican highway within sight of the U.S. border, the eight families began handing out their burritos, coffee and fresh water several times during the week. Sometimes Mexican police or the military chased them off. Often there were undercover Mexican police agents watching the families distribute the food to make sure they were not selling the burritos and beverages.

Peg and a pilgrim at the *comedor*.

The activities of passing out food and water were surrounded by an air of foreboding, and the families were made to feel that somehow they were breaking the law.

As the numbers of migrants increased, more help was needed. A local Mexican high school became involved and brought rice and beans to this spot under the bridge. The eight families talked with a local priest from Christ the

King Catholic Parish, asking for help. Sister Engracia Robles became involved, and after being chased and harassed for providing humanitarian care to recently deported migrants, she approached the mayor of Nogales. He generously offered to rent a small piece of land on the major highway near the Mariposa port of entry, and this hillside location became the place known as the *comedor,* the Aid Center for Deported Migrants.

Lupita Flores, a kitchen chef at the *comedor,* relates that meals began to be served at the shelter in January 2008. Initially, things were primitive and services were basic at the *comedor.* There was no sewer line. There was a desperate need for the safe preparation of food and for sanitation facilities with sinks, toilets and adequate drainage. The numbers of migrants seeking assistance continued to mount. There was a shelter for migrants named San Juan Bosco, in another part of town. If the shelters were full, many would take refuge at night in a cemetery near the *comedor.* These displaced refugees were and continue to be some of the most vulnerable, forgotten people in this hemisphere.

In 2007 and 2008, representatives of the California Province of the Society of Jesus (Jesuits) and Jesuit Refugee Service/USA did a needs assessment for a migrant ministry along the Arizona/Sonora border. They learned of the need for a binational migrant ministry that would work in the areas of humanitarian aid, education and research/advocacy.

The Kino Border Initiative (KBI) was officially launched in two phases. In May 2008, the comedor became part of the KBI and Nazareth House (*Casa Nazaret*), a shelter for women and children. Here, the Missionary Sisters of the Eucharist created a safe space to protect women and children from the threats of the street. The migrant women could sleep in safety, bathe and talk with the sisters about their experiences.

The KBI as a whole was inaugurated in January of 2009. What is unusual about the KBI is the fact that it is a binational ministry of six organizations: Jesuit Refugee Service/USA in Washington, D.C., the California Province of the Society of Jesus, the Mexican Province of the Society of Jesus, the Missionary Sisters of the Eucharist, the Archdiocese of Hermosillo and the Diocese of Tucson. This collaborative effort has created a place of safety for thousands of refugees, while the *comedor* has evolved into an efficient humanitarian aid station providing food for the body and spiritual sustenance for the soul. The KBI is doing courageous frontline work in the face of discord in Mexico and controversy in the United States.

—*mm*—

On a cold January day, I focus on a young woman who is limping. She is sitting in the first-aid station located across the street with Nurse Norma, the Mexican nurse who runs this clinic like a well-oiled machine. The injured woman tells us she was pushed roughly into a truck yesterday by a U.S. Border Patrol agent and cannot bear weight on her left leg. The hip area is black and blue with a large bruise, and there are abrasions on her thigh and ankles. A young man standing in the small waiting area offers to take this woman to the hospital. She needs

X-rays. He whisks her away toward downtown Nogales in a dented pickup truck.

A few hours later I see this young woman again. Now she has a leg brace and crutches and is smiling. Mexico has a universal health-care system for Mexican nationals. She shows me a bottle of pain pills as she enters the *comedor* for some breakfast. A priest tells me the young man who drove her to the hospital is a *coyote*. There are good guys in this business, but there are also nefarious thugs who prey on migrants. This fellow is a good guy today. He helped a young woman get some needed medical treatment. I can only hope there are no strings attached.

The going rate for *coyotes* to guide a group across the desert in 2011 is $3,000. A few years ago it was $1,000. Thanks to the increased presence of Homeland Security in our desert, the *coyotes* are making more money than ever. When the journey is more dangerous, the price goes up. Somehow the migrants come up with the money.

The increased presence of Border Patrol agents and ICE has driven the migrant crossers farther into rugged, isolated parts of the Sonoran Desert as they make their way toward Tucson and Phoenix. The *coyotes* promise safe passage for the migrants but often become lost themselves as they try to guide their groups to the United States. Telling the migrant groups that it is an easy walk to Tucson—two days tops—the crossers are ill-prepared for the arduous journey ahead.

I learn that the *coyotes* and drug smugglers are not allowed in the *comedor* for meals or counsel with the Jesuits. *Coyotes* often stand outside the shelter recruiting for their next journey into the desert and across the border. I see men in pickup trucks parked nearby, always on their cell phones, watching the activity around the *comedor*. When the migrants leave the safety of the shelter for the day, they are vulnerable to the forces around them. They are easy to spot, with their backpacks, hoodies and bedrolls.

A few weeks later I observe something that puzzles me. Arriving on this particular morning at the *comedor*, a young man in a bright red shirt immediately asks me for food and money. He wears a shiny gold chain with a crucifix around his neck. He speaks very little English, so I struggle to understand his request. He is insistent that I hear his predicament.

"They will not let me into the *comedor* for food. I am very hungry." He looks clean-shaven and sports an expensive new red polo shirt, and I am having a disconnect here. The well-worn clothes and dusty jeans of the migrants are not evident with this fellow. He is wearing a designer-label shirt and gold jewelry.

Milling around the shelter are men and women with babies scoping out the bags of donated clothing and supplies in our van. It is the usual mayhem and confusion and desperation—people asking for toothbrushes, soap, blankets, jackets. The man in the red shirt appears to be an outsider. People are avoiding him.

"How come this man isn't allowed to eat with the others?" I ask Francisco, a novice priest-in-training.

"This man is a *coyote*," he tells me. "The women are afraid of him." Taking me aside, Francisco whispers, "He is recruiting. It is complicated. We cannot allow him to come into this shelter."

So I busy myself sorting piles of clothes, finding the

toothbrushes and generally doing my best to avoid eye contact with the man in the bright red shirt standing outside the door.

Five minutes later, I see Padre Francisco carrying out a steaming plate of food for the red-shirted *coyote*. He sits on the sidewalk in the midst of the commotion around him and devours the beans and rice and vegetables. He inhales a glass of milk. Francisco places his hand on the fellow's head, a sort of blessing. Neither one speaks.

I ask Francisco about this later in the day. "Why did you feed him?"

He just remarks, "Even *coyotes* need food."

Francisco is right. It is a complicated business.

IN THE TRENCHES

It is easy to miss the *comedor* when driving by this busy Mexican highway. There are no offices or executive suites. People get their hands dirty here. Coming to work in baseball caps and sweatshirts and flowered aprons, the priests and nuns swab out the toilets, count the numbers lined up at the door, peel endless bags of potatoes and keep a stray cat in residence to quell the mouse population. There is a peculiar mix of chaos and order and respect in this place where they feed and care for hundreds of people each day.

The *comedor* is the stage for some of the most politically provocative work done on the border. Jesuit priests of the KBI and the Missionary Sisters of the Eucharist make this special place happen. Their mission is to serve the people

Comedor kitty in the sun.

who suffer from contemporary American immigration policy.

It was several weeks of visits to *el comedor* before I realized that the men who organized the masses of migrants lined up in front of the shelter were priests. The women who were serving the food and chopping the vegetables were Sisters of the Eucharist. These people didn't look like your average priest or nun. They mingled with the migrants, sitting with them quietly during breakfast and dinner. The sisters wore colorful aprons and zipped up and down the aisles ladling out beans, tortillas and love to these lost souls.

"Lost" is an understatement. Many migrants deported in the past twenty-four hours have no idea where they are.

Nogales? We show them this border city on a map and point out where their own home is—Chiapas, Veracruz, Guatemala, El Salvador.

I listen to the stories the migrants tell me of their experience, and try to look into their eyes and offer some support. The suffering here is the most palpable pain I have ever witnessed. The disappointment is profound. Most of the migrants have never heard of Nogales, Mexico.

I point to a map taped to the wall and try to explain the mileage to New York City or Chicago. There is a lack of comprehension about the distances. For many, the information falls on deaf ears. If a young man has not seen his parents or siblings in two years, it doesn't matter if there are thousands of miles to traverse. The dangers of the desert and the presence of Border Patrol are minor impediments. The migrants politely listen to me and my stories of the risky business of travel across the Sonoran Desert. They unfailingly thank me for the food and friendship on this busy morning and ask if I have clean socks or a backpack in our stash of clothing. Then they are out the door.

Many of them will try to cross into the United States despite the dangers. How bad can it be? Most have suffered greatly just getting to the border.

Frequently the Samaritans succeed in persuading travelers to turn back and return to their home villages in Mexico. We dig into our pockets for money to buy food and bus tickets for a migrant's long ride home to a village a thousand miles away.

"Please, take this necklace that I made last night in the shelter," says a young woman who gives me a beaded rosary she has fashioned while contemplating her next step. She is returning to her village in the mountains of Oaxaca, looking exhausted and disillusioned.

There is a bittersweet moment when we purchase a bus ticket. The migrants have a look of defeat on their faces, and I feel like I am barely scratching the surface of their disappointment and despair. There are hugs and thank-yous as they board the bus for the long ride home. Their eyes stare past me with glazed emptiness as they wonder what their future holds back in Chiapas or Veracruz or Oaxaca.

THE CAST

There are miracles afoot every Tuesday when I cross the line. The priests and the good Sisters of the Eucharist do God's work. There is no better religion than this. The parade of people who make this place hum are worthy of mention. The characters in this cast are my heroes.

One of my favorites is Francisco, a priest-in-training from Mexico City. He bustles around the *comedor* wearing a sort of carpenter's apron full of pencils and paper. I watch him helping migrants with deportation documents and identification papers. Mexican bureaucracy, like most bureaucracies, is a muddled mass of triplicate papers and confusion.

I first notice Francisco going about his daily housekeeping tasks: sweeping the floor, swabbing out the toilets and pouring Ajax into the sinks. I have no idea that he is a Jesuit spending time here as part of his preparation to be a priest. Francisco is hands-on. He dives into the messy business of keeping the shelter operating with zeal as he strives for efficiency and order. Privately he tells me that when things are hectic and disorganized, he has to take a deep breath or it drives him crazy.

I watch him scurry off with a broom in his hand.

Francisco struggles with his English just as I struggle with my Spanish. We bond around our mutual inability to speak the other's native tongue. He looks a bit like Jesus, at least the Jesus image in the Bible I had as a child. Francisco sports a beard and his hair is pulled back in a ponytail. He has a face of kindness and patience.

I see him sitting at the long picnic tables in the shelter, talking quietly to migrants. Sometimes I watch as he feeds the stray cat that has taken up residence. Francisco and Father Martín, a Jesuit priest, act like gentle nightclub bouncers at the doorway of the *comedor*. Only those with proper immigration papers[1] are allowed in for meals and clothes. They are very strict about this. You are either "in" and allowed to eat the wonderful food or you are "out" on the sidewalk. If you are out in the cold, you might be a *coyote*, or a local homeless person, a pimp, maybe a drug dealer. Francisco and Martín run a tight ship.

Francisco left the *comedor* after a year of service to continue his training at another posting in Mexico. Before he left I tried to tell Francisco how much his daily work had touched my heart. The language obstacles got in the way and felt like the gigantic wall on the border. We crossed the metaphoric border between us and clambered over the wall of words.

"It's like this," Francisco tells me. "We are all like a giant orchestra, with God as the director." He sees all of us—the aid workers, the migrants, the drug dealers, the military—as players on a stage. Francisco believes that we are all playing a part, often stumbling and making mistakes but continually trying to create some sort of music, however dissonant and raucous the sound. It is a good analogy for what goes on here.

———

Father Martín McIntosh is the daily overseer directing the action at the *comedor* and is a Jesuit of the Mexican Province. He is the gatekeeper as he stands at the door and allows the migrants who have the proper immigration papers to enter one by one. Putting his hand on each person's shoulder, he welcomes them to this place of safety and nourishment.

When Father Martín offers a prayer of grace before the morning meal, the intensity in the room is unequivocal. Every head is bowed. The silence is absolute. I think about my own inability in most church settings to pay attention to a prayer: I wiggle, I play with the hymnal, I space out and think about other things. The migrants are hungry, exhausted, dusty, trail-worn and often in pain. And yet they are in total connection with the moment of prayer.

The priest prays for the safety of these travelers and for their reuniting with families. Many weep during the moment of prayer. It is a touching and profound beginning to a day at the *comedor*.

———

Father Sean Carroll is another major player in the drama of the KBI. Sean is from Boston but spent his formative years in California. As executive director of the KBI, he oversees the humanitarian efforts, providing education and research opportunities to visiting academics and others seeking to understand what is going on in the borderlands. I have seen Sean pass out piles of tortillas on sweltering days at the *comedor* and later lead a discussion with educators and politicians from all over the world. He articulates the issues of migration—the trafficking, the drugs, the abuse, the inhumanity—without mincing words.

Once at a social gathering about border issues, Sean told me that living on the border and doing this kind of work had been the furthest thing from his mind as a younger Jesuit priest.

"I fought it for a long time," he tells me. But this is a place that brings out his commitment and passion.

—◆—

I have watched nurse Norma Quijada function in stifling heat and frigid cold at the first-aid station in Mexico. Her organization skills and calm demeanor when confronted with a line of immigrants and a long list of complaints leaves me in awe. She will simultaneously care for blistered feet, infections from cactus thorns and unchecked diabetes. The Samaritans and other nonprofit organizations supply her small clinic with electrolyte powders and water-purification tablets for desert journeys as well as bandages and ointments for infected wounds. Norma is compassion and efficiency in action, and the migrants are deeply appreciative of her ministrations.

—◆—

Leonard Cohen, a poet who touched my heart back in the 1960's, composed a song called "Sisters of Mercy".[2] The tune speaks of benevolent women—the sisters—who are there when you cannot take one more step. They are tender and merciful and catch you when you fall.

I think of this song each time I watch the Sisters of the Eucharist in action. They never sit still. Besides serving the meals at the *comedor*, they direct activities at *Casa Nazaret* a few blocks away, with beds for women and children. Sister Rosalba lights up a room with her incredible smile and warmth. Another nun, Sister Lorena, always plays salsa music on a small CD player during mealtime. I've seen her dancing up and down the aisles, raising the spirit of this place with song and joy. Sister Engracia Robles exudes wisdom and grace when she presides over a meal.

All the sisters are dedicated to the prevention of abuse of women and children. Many migrants squirm when the sisters speak of the harm that abuse toward women brings to children and to a relationship. These women are faith in action.

FEEDING THE BODY AND SOUL

Approaching the *comedor* most mornings after walking a mile through the dusty construction site of the border wall, I work up an appetite. The smells emanating from the tiny kitchen as breakfast is being dished up are one of my favorite moments in the day. There are prayers of thanksgiving and prayers for the safety of these pilgrims. Then the music

Lorena and the peppers.

begins and the plates are passed up and down the long tables. The cuisine is hearty and exceptional. Beans, Mexican rice and usually a meat-and-vegetable stew (*cocido*) or stir-fry is on a typical menu. Tortillas are piled high, and bowls of salsa line the tables.

A volunteer kitchen crew creates the colorful, nutritious feasts. Lupita, one of the original aid workers in this special place, knows how to cook delicious food in large quantities. Nothing fancy, but it is real food. None of the packaged stuff. The women who create these dishes are volunteers from the local Catholic church. They can be seen mixing, ladling, scooping up and serving in an eight-by-ten-foot work space. Moving like a choreographed ballet, they are able to feed a hundred or more migrants every morning and evening.

While the women in the kitchen are busy dishing up this hearty fare, Samaritans queue up in an assembly line and pass out plates of beans and rice, with a bit of meat on the side. Local farmers donate fresh *calabasas* (squash), tomatoes, eggplant, *chiles*, and tortillas, and the good ladies in the kitchen create smells straight from heaven. Sometimes there is a spicy *mole* sauce for the chicken. Often there is a green *chile* sauce for the pork.

I make a pest of myself in this kitchen trying to figure out how these women can create these delicious meals with such ease. They have things down to a precise dance, wearing their colorful aprons as they expertly dish up the fare. I often think of my own mother when I watch these women in the kitchen. How she would have loved to join them in the cooking, the serving, the cleanup, and the chopping and peeling for the next meal.

One time the cooks created a *mole*-and-chicken dish that was the most delicious meal I have had in Mexico. Period.

It was noon, time for lunch, and I was ravenously hungry.

"So how do you do that? How do you make the *mole* sauce with the chocolate and the spices?" I asked, staring at the huge cauldron of thick bubbling goodness.

One of the cooks ladled me a dish of rice, chicken and the rich coffee-colored sauce.

It was all there—the fusion of the spices, the raisins, the chocolate and the chilies simmered together into a sauce that was complex and piquant. It's all about the sauce when you enjoy *mole* poured over chicken and rice. I still think about sampling that dish on a wintry day in January. Sitting in the damp chill of the *comedor,* it both saved me and caught me unawares. How can this gourmet dish exist in this humble little shelter on the coldest day of winter? It fortified me and I'm sure gave strength to the large group of migrants at the evening meal.

Food is more than calories. These ladies know this. Their dishes are simple and amazing and are devoured with gratitude and gusto every day.

Plus, they dance. As the meal is being served and the immigrants are eating their fill, the Samaritans and the kitchen crew can be seen sashaying up and down the aisles in a wild *merengue.* The beat is hot, and so is the food. There may be despair here at *el comedor,* but the music and dance provide a welcome craziness that defies logic. When things look bleak, it doesn't hurt to dance.

One memorable time, it was difficult to sit still, as the music was loud and furiously captivating. Everyone was tapping toes and swaying back and forth.

─⌇⌇─

A handsome young man tangos up the aisle, leaving his breakfast on his plate, and grabs one of the Samaritans in a wild salsa bit of merry-making. The whole room lights up and there is cheering, clapping and noise-making as these two execute some fancy footwork. Everyone stops eating and watches this display of unadulterated, uninhibited movement.

How can this be? Ten minutes ago we were praying. Now we're dancing. We're in a room of more than one hundred migrants who have faced the Sonoran Desert in December, and have been dumped into this little border town. And here we are dancing, eating some great food and making crazy hooting noises in this humble lean-to of a shelter.

—*mn*—

I remember my visits to the migrant camps as a public health nurse in Oregon many years ago. People from Mexico and Central America traveled to the Pacific Northwest to pick fruit in the lush orchards of Oregon and Washington. Preparing traditional food reminiscent of the villages of Mexico created a domestic center for the nomadic lives of the migrant fruit-pickers. The women provided this anchor, and life was better because of it. A bubbling pot of pinto beans reminded the migrants of home.

The price of groceries in Mexico is often higher than in the United States. Feeding several hundred people twice a day at *el comedor* takes some ingenuity and frugality.

Always there are bowls of salsa and piles of homemade tortillas on the long tables during meals. The salsa is fiery and a necessary condiment in the Mexican diet. There is no mild salsa at the *comedor*. Mild is for gringos. I watch as one of the kitchen volunteers makes a huge cauldron of *chile salsa*. My eyes water as I smell the fragrant spicy chilies bubbling in the cooking pot. Requests for *"Mas salsa, por favor"* are frequently heard each morning as the Samaritans ladle out bowl after bowl for the hungry travelers.

CHAPTER TWO

Spring

The weather becomes more hospitable for migrant travel as spring comes to southern Arizona. One night in March there was a full moon, the largest and brightest moon of the year. The desert was glowing. The blooming agaves looked like candles dotting the desert expanse. Coyotes howled and owls hooted. Lines of javelina paraded past our home rooting for cacti, waking our dogs.

I lie awake on nights like this thinking about migrants traveling across the desert in the moonlight. There is no need for flashlights when the moon illuminates the desert floor. It is daylight at midnight.

My guess is that Latino travelers migrate north in record numbers when the weather accommodates their journey. The numbers at *el comedor* continue to be larger than usual. Often there are 150 pilgrims lined up in the morning. Breakfast is served in two shifts, as the small shelter can hold only about one hundred at a sitting. Women and children sit together at the long tables on these mornings. The men sit

A dance of joy.

separately as they wait for breakfast to be served. The nights are still quite cold, but the days are just about perfect, with temperatures hovering in the seventies. Jackets with fleecy linings are needed at night, but it is T-shirt weather during the day.

The Sisters of the Eucharist discuss with me the needs of the women—underwear and sanitary napkins.

I think about this. Trekking across a desert wilderness with an unexpected menstrual period and no feminine supplies to get me through the next five days—well, the thought makes me shudder. In fact, just hiking for days without a flush toilet or menstrual supplies, cramps and all, is just another nightmare my migrant friends face. Then there is the lack of privacy while tending to these intimate personal needs, often in the company of exploitive, hardened guides who prey on the women. I put out the word to a few women friends and soon I have a carful of underwear, sanitary napkins and tampons.

Ask and ye shall receive.

We spread out the panties and tampons on a separate table at the *comedor* for the women. They are gone in a flash. Such a little thing, and yet these basic items are such a comfort for women trying to reach *el norte*.

WE'RE IN THIS TOGETHER

We walk to *el comedor,* having parked our cars on the U.S. side near the border, and wind our way through the building equipment and road graders that are part of the expansion of border security. The construction workers are often friendly and curious about our little group with the red Samaritan hats and T-shirts displaying our motto: "Humanitarian Aid Is Never a Crime."

One day I have an encounter on the walk back to my car on the U.S. side. It is one of those experiences that hits me broadside. A large, brawny Mexican-American fellow in full Homeland Security regalia makes eye contact as I walk through the U.S. Customs border check back toward my car. Tipping the scales at 275 pounds or more, he looks me straight in the eye as I greet him with *"Buenos días."* He is a U.S. Customs officer, laden with a Kevlar vest, a breast shield and an assault weapon slung over his dark blue uniform. As he stands at attention with his rifle, sweat pours off his forehead.

He motions to me to step toward him. Quietly and tentatively he asks, "What do you do over there?" pointing toward the *comedor.*

So I tell him.

"We bring clothes, medical supplies and a listening ear to the people who have been deported. There were more than one hundred migrants waiting for us this morning."

I continue to tell him that I am a nurse, and so I personally take care of wounds and upper respiratory infections at a small first-aid station. My Samaritan friends walking behind me now join in the conversation. Rarely does Homeland Security engage us in discourse, and this fellow is definitely reaching out.

It is a special moment. I have so many questions yet can think of nothing to say. I am cowed by the weaponry and the uniform yet touched by his interest.

A Samaritan colleague asks the officer, "Why do you wear that?" pointing to a thick breastplate. He invites me to touch the breastplate and the back plate as well. The officer explains that he has over forty pounds of equipment and protective clothing. Pointing to the hills surrounding his station, he says, "We are always being watched by the drug cartels. Always. I watch them. They watch me."

He is matter-of-fact about this. Holding a pair of binoculars in his hand, he focuses on the surrounding hills. I gaze up at the mountains and see nothing. Our officer insists they are there, probably hiding today but often just standing on the hillside watching him. He tells us that the cartels check to see who is on duty for Homeland Security and then decide when to smuggle a "load" over the wall into the United States.

"Really? So some officers are easier to sneak by than others?" I ask.

Our officer friend does not answer this question.

As we turn to leave, he says to us, "God bless you for what you do." Loudly.

We are all stunned.

At times our relationships with Homeland Security have been adversarial. I have gotten the feeling that immigration officials think that Samaritans get in the way of the "real work," catching terrorists and drug runners. In point of fact, there have been no alleged terrorists apprehended on the U.S.-Mexican border. *Nada.*

As we continue our walk back into the United States, we feel a camaraderie with this fellow, with his guns, his shields and his watchful eyes looking toward the mountains. I wondered if he had relatives in Mexico.

It is so easy for me to fall into the clichés about Homeland Security:

"They are going to extremes."

"They hate Mexicans."

"They are not humane or fair in their treatment of migrants."

"It feels like a police state."

"They see things in black and white."

"They are so full of machismo, with their guns, their authority ..."

And on and on and on.

Now I remember Mr. U.S. Customs Officer, the man who asked God's blessing for the work that we do. He is Homeland Security and he is doing his job, safeguarding the peace. We are the peacemakers. It is never black or white, right or wrong, good or bad, but shades of all of it.

UNSUNG HEROES

Spring in the Sonoran Desert is a time for renewal and hope. The open-range cattle take command of the roads around our ranch and they are a nuisance, but also a lively piece of the Old West. And then there are the babies, all the little calves that kick up their heels and chase after my car, only to come to a skidding stop and run for their mothers. I can't help smiling when I drive back home from Mexico in the spring.

Showing up at *el comedor* each week feels like spitting into the wind at times. Sometimes I get it right in the face. In terms of making some kind of impact on immigration policy, I feel like I should be doing more. But what is more? The problems of global suffering are huge. Should I stop doing my little piece at the *comedor* because the whole issue is so unmanageable? My friends tell me that we should solve the problems of our own country first. There is plenty of poverty and suffering right here in the U.S.A.

True.

But now it is spring. Things always look better in spring. Birds are nesting again under the eaves of our porch. The calves are hopelessly happy and frisky. The Samaritans may not be saving the world or getting the attention of the president about immigration policy, but we are showing up each week.

Mexico is my neighbor. This is not a time to close our hearts but a time to open them to those who are asking for very little, really. They want to work, and they want safe passage to the land of plenty. *Los Estados Unidos.*

These are my brothers and sisters, and they live right around the corner, on the other side of the fence.

—~~~—

One morning I meet Rudolfo at the *comedor,* a man from Mazatlán. His English is perfect. He tells me he was picked up in the desert after eight days of wandering. He was part of a group trying to make the journey on foot to Tucson, and a woman and two children who were part of the entourage could not keep up. The *coyote* told the group to leave the woman and her children behind, as they had to keep up the brisk pace through the rough terrain.

Rudolfo could not leave the woman or her struggling family, and so he stayed behind with them, carrying both the woman and sometimes the children on his back. They survived on a few candy bars and two bottles of water. After three days of wandering, the woman and the children arrived at a safe place, but Rudolfo was picked up by the Border Patrol. He sacrificed his own chance to reach a safe destination in the United States for the deliverance of the woman he had carried for days.

When I touch his back in a gesture of comfort, I feel a bulge underneath his shirt. Dressings cover a serious open flesh wound that has developed after days of carrying this small helpless family. He brushes off this injury as minor, but half of his back is covered with dressings protecting the draining wound. In his pocket is a bottle of antibiotics. Nurse Norma has plied her skills well, treating this injury at the first-aid station.

I ask Rudolfo about his plans. He will return to Mazatlán, where his wife and three children wait for him. There are tears as he speaks of them. Rudolfo tells me he had a successful kayaking business two years ago and worked with a cruise-ship line, taking tourists on whale-watching and sea-kayaking excursions. Then came the robberies and shootings in Mazatlán in the past two years, and several cruise ships canceled their stopovers in this port of call. Rudolfo is unable to support his family without the cruise ships. This is why he tried to cross into the United States.

He tells me he will return to his home in Mazatlán and later spend a week or more in Puerto Vallarta, hoping to discover another way to develop his kayaking business. Puerto Vallarta is still a popular port of call for the big cruise ships. He shows me a card that says he is also a certified scuba dive instructor and tells me he is eager to set up his business where there are tourists and safety.

He unwraps the photos of his children, which he has hidden in his jeans, and his eyes fill again. The photos are bent and worn, obviously handled many times during these past weeks.

"I am lucky to be alive. I know this. I just want to go home."

MOTHER'S DAY

Spring means Mother's Day, one of those Hallmark events that evoke a whole range of emotions. Good memories, bad times, nostalgia and sadness. For me there is always guilt. Guilt that I'm not with my own kids on this day. Guilt that I didn't do the whole motherhood thing better. There is also for me a low-level anxiety that no one will remember that today is Mother's Day. The kids won't call. My husband will forget.

I smile when I remember the kids growing up in our big old rambling Victorian house in Oregon. The house had its quirks, but it seemed to embrace us as a family. And on Mother's Day I could hear the kids giggling and scurrying in the kitchen as they made me breakfast, which they would serve on a tray complete with some flowers in a jelly glass and coffee with whipped cream on top. Their specialty was crepes, with strawberries and mountains of whipped cream. They would pile on the bed with me along with their gourmet Mother's Day treats. The coffee would slosh around and they would watch me carefully as I tasted their offerings. They were so pleased with themselves, and I was so happy to be in this place with them.

Now they are parents themselves, so I wonder if they will have breakfast in bed with whipped cream and a messy kitchen and lots of giggles and flowers and all of it. I call them on Mother's Day, and yes, they are in the thick of it. I smile at the revelry I can hear in their own homes. Lots of shrieks and carrying on.

I think about my last visit to the *comedor*. There were a few women, one or two kids and a lot of men gazing vacantly into space as they sat at the long tables for breakfast.

—ᴍᴍ—

One man is slumped over at the table, staring at his plate of beans and rice. He is not touching the food. Looking pale and sick, he rocks back and forth on the bench.

"Are you OK?" I ask in my halting Spanish.

In perfect English he tells me, "I've just gotten out of the hospital and I'm not supposed to have anything but liquids for a few days." He cannot yet tolerate solid food.

His name is Jonathan, and he has been lost in the desert for two days without food or water, abandoned by his *coyote* because he couldn't keep up. Drinking the water from cattle troughs, he began to have stomach cramps and to vomit early in his journey to *el norte*. He was lagging behind his group of nine travelers. So they left him.

The Border Patrol found him asleep on the desert floor.

"They saved my life," he said. He was taken to a detention center and then transported to the University Medical Center in Tucson, where he was treated for dehydration and exposure.

Wearing the drawstring pants from the hospital and a threadbare T-shirt, he holds his stomach and rocks back and forth at the table. His feet are bound in gauze bandages, and his skin has a pale yellow cast. The man is ill, and the beans and rice simply will not do this morning. The kitchen crew gives me a glass of milk for my new friend, Jonathan, and he takes some tentative sips as he continues telling me his story.

He had been working in Seattle for seven years as an electrician, a job that pays well and one that he enjoyed. Money was sent home regularly to his wife, his three children and his mother, all in Veracruz. His daughter's *quinceañera* (her fifteenth birthday, a celebration of womanhood in Mexico) was coming up and she begged him to be there for this special day. He was given a four-month leave of absence from his Seattle job and went home to celebrate.

Trying to get back to Seattle was a different story. After his failed attempt to cross the border and his near-death experience in the desert, he was returned to a detention center in the United States where his clothes, wallet, ID, cell phone and money disappeared. The man had literally nothing but the hospital-issued clothes on his back.

He wants to go home to Veracruz, be with his family and get well. And here is the silver lining to the story: The Mexican Consulate will pay for this man's bus ticket home because he is disabled and is still in a fragile state. The Samaritans help Jonathan obtain a bus ticket and expedite the transportation paperwork so he can return to Veracruz. And we find him a clean polo shirt for the trip home.

I think about Jonathan and this life-changing experience. All he wants at this moment is to go home to his wife and "live like a real family." Risking his life to make the comfortable wages of an electrician in Seattle—well, it is not how he will live his life. He will figure out a way to survive economically in Veracruz and celebrate all his children's birthdays and *quinceañeras.*

I'm missing my own mother and wishing she could come with me on my treks down to Mexico each week. My mother died several years back, but she is in my thoughts a lot. She would disapprove of the civil-disobedience aspects of my immigration politics but would be the first to lend a hand to the hungry and the wounded. My mother was both a kissing mother and a scolding mother, and I got generous amounts of both. I think she would both kiss and scold at the *comedor*—scold the migrants for leaving their children but kiss all the children and wish them godspeed on their journey. She would bake cookies for the travelers and bring loaves of her signature banana bread. If the migrants were going to cross, they would be stocked with her homemade confections. And prayers.

I try to imagine leaving my children in one country and traveling under the radar to another country, knowing I am not welcome, despised by many and might never see my family again. To be totally vulnerable with little or no money, no job, trekking across the searing desert in May, hoping for a chance to make a few dollars—it all sounds like a nightmare.

It *is* a nightmare.

Jonathan survived the nightmare, but barely. I wish I could be in Veracruz when that bus pulls into his village and his family greets him. The whole scenario makes me smile.

His mother will kiss him and scold him. I just know it.

ALFONSO'S STORY

Sometimes I sit on the patio at our home in the desert and watch the ants. They march in long lines across rocks and dusty creek beds known as *arroyos* like a faceless army. When a few get crushed and killed, the rest march right over them. There doesn't seem to be any awareness of losing a comrade. The march goes on.

It's different with elephants. I've read that they gather around their dead in a ritual of respect. But this sort of consciousness is primarily the stuff of humans. We care. We honor life. We help those who are struggling to survive.

So I think about life and death when I speak with my migrant friends. I tell them of the dangers of the desert, the many miles of hard travel it takes to reach a city, the many liters of water they will need to survive. They smile politely and look away.

There is a force stronger than logic when it comes to returning to family. I know many will try to cross no matter what the odds. They search for decent shoes and backpacks in our piles of clothes and supplies. Many wear large crosses around their necks. The men thank me and are unfailingly polite. Then they are gone.

One bright April morning I meet Alfonso, a family man from Vista, California, a medium-sized town in north San Diego County, where he and his wife have five children. He limps across the shelter on blistered feet, carrying his breakfast of beans and rice. Alfonso tells me he was a butcher for twenty years until he lost his job due to his immigration status. For the last two years he did pickup work. He got by. But he caught a bad break.

He was arrested at a neighborhood market in Vista while minding the store as a favor for the owner. A sheriff's deputy came in with new synthetic drug regulations that required a signature. It was a simple bureaucratic transaction. Alfonso signed and when asked for identification, all he could produce was his Mexican *matrícula consular* (Mexican identification).

Alfonso was deported to Tijuana, tried to cross back into the United States, spent time in a detention center and was deported again to Nogales, Mexico.

When I meet him, both feet are chewed up, with open blisters from many days of walking. Wrapped in gauze and bandages, his feet won't fit into shoes, so I find him slippers to wear over his injuries. His friend Isaac stands nearby that morning, helping Alfonso manage the breakfast plates, the coffee, the bustle of the shelter. I warn Alfonso about the dangers of the desert. There is a glaze over his eyes. He doesn't hear a word. But I figure if the man can't walk across the room, he won't try walking across the desert.

I am wrong.

Alfonso began his journey home to Vista three days later, on April 20. By the second day, he couldn't keep up with his group. The *coyote* guide abandoned him and pushed on. Isaac stayed behind with his friend. Finding a cell phone in Alfonso's pocket, Isaac hiked two hours, climbing a steep hill to get cell reception and called 911. The two were somewhere on the Tohono O'odham Reservation, a vast desert expanse of more than four thousand square miles. At last Isaac was able to reach a Border Patrol agent and begged him to return to the place where he'd left Alfonso. The agent promptly arrested him.

I was not there to hear what was said between the Border Patrol agent and Isaac. According to a newspaper report, Isaac wanted to immediately guide the Border Patrol to his injured friend. A two-hour walk away. The agent refused. He said the Border Patrol would mount a search.

Isaac was deported to Mexicali after several days in a U.S. detention center. It was only upon his release days later that the Border Patrol requested that Isaac take them to the spot where he last saw Alfonso. The agents needed Isaac's help in finding his friend. Isaac called Alfonso's wife in Vista, who immediately set up an altar and prayed for her husband's safety.

On April 26, Isaac led the Border Patrol directly to his friend. He found Alfonso at the base of Baboquivari, the sacred mountain of the Tohono O'odham, a Native American tribe in southeastern Arizona. Alfonso had not survived. His body was in such an advanced state of decomposition that it took the medical examiner several days to identify it.

There was no local news coverage of this death in the desert. I found out about Alfonso's death in the *North County Times,* a newspaper from Alfonso's town of Vista, California.[3] When I got the news, I called the Border Patrol to find out what had really happened out there in the desert. The public relations officer was cordial and helpful to a point but told me repeatedly that I didn't "have all the information." Which is correct. This is why

I called the agency. After all, it is unthinkable to me that a law enforcement officer would not look for an injured person at the mercy of desert temperatures in the triple digits.

"You don't know the whole story, ma'am," the public relations officer told me with a trace of weariness in his voice. "There's more to it than what you read in the papers."

"You're absolutely right. I don't know the whole story," I countered. "That is why I'm calling you. Isn't part of your mandate to save people who are injured and lost in the desert?"

Our conversation went back and forth for several minutes. I got nowhere with this agent.

So what happened? Why did Alfonso die when he could have been rescued? Perhaps it is like the ants marching over the bodies of their dead to get their ant jobs done.

"People are tired of all the news about death in the desert," the agent patiently explained. "They want to hear about capturing drug smugglers. They want stories of decapitated heads in the desert."

The guy was trying to cover his ass.

Most of the time my conversations and encounters with Border Patrol agents have been helpful and cordial. I have felt a mutual respect. Many agents have told me they are happy to have the help of Samaritans when searching for lost or injured migrants. I am grateful that the agents are in the business of saving lives and keeping the peace.

But there was no reason for this death.

America's irrational immigration policies are taking a toll on us as a nation. We have lost our moral compass.

DESERT SEARCHES

During the spring, I went on some desert searches with Samaritans. After packing up the van with medical supplies, water, food packs and clothing, we set off into the backcountry where there are known migrant trails. The country is vast and beautiful during the late spring, with the color of blooming cacti and the soaring of migrating birds distracting us from the job at hand. The bees are in a frenzy as they drink deeply of the crimson and golden blossoms on the cacti and mesquite trees. The buzzing and darting of the bees is a fertile sound of abundance. The nectars flow freely.

Birds migrate, people migrate, butterflies migrate. Arizona is a crossroads for living things on the move. We are a nation of nomads, with our RVs, campgrounds and outdoor adventures.

In May, temperatures reach into the nineties and begin to creep into triple digits. It is eighty-five degrees at 9 a.m. and climbing.

"There is a lot of activity out there," a Border Patrol agent reports to our van of Samaritan searchers. We gaze through binoculars and see nothing but the birds and flowering saguaros, their white waxy flowers looking like Easter bonnets. I think about who might be out there but see only the twisting trails up and down the mountains. The Border Patrol agent tells me that the migrants travel at night and you can see their flashlights in long ribbons dotting the desert.

"It looks like an L.A. freeway."

Because the U.S.-Mexican border has become a militarized zone of Border Patrol and U.S. marshals, all heavily armed and ready to pursue the undocumented entrants,

Harry Smith and Ricardo Osburn on a water drop.

the migrants have been driven farther into the desert. The country is rugged, and towns and ranches are few and far between. Migrants are easily lost, disoriented and are often abandoned by their *coyotes*. Carrying enough food and water is a huge challenge, even for the young and hardy. Over 2,200 migrants have died in the Sonoran desert since 2000. There are undoubtedly more, as these figures represent only the bodies that have been found. The desert is vast; many bodies remain lost and may never be found.

One of them was found in the Santa Cruz River, not too far from my desert home. The medical examiner thought the male was between sixteen and twenty years of age. The story is poignant.

It is May, and things are beginning to heat up. The Border Patrol receives a call on a cell phone from a migrant.

"I have found a dead body," the migrant says in heavily accented English. "It is in the river."

The migrant tries to describe the location, which is a challenge because the man does not know the landmarks or exactly where he is. He does his best and describes a riverbed, a large rock and a village. It sounds like the body is in the Santa Cruz River, near Elephant Head rock, north of the village of Tubac, Arizona.

Then there is an unexpected storm, with pelting rain and hail. Searchers go into the area after the rain has abated and for two days cannot find the body. Finally a Samaritan on a desert search discovers the victim quite a distance from the original location of death. The body has washed downstream. The migrant has been dead for several days, and no identification or cell phone was evident. The young man died of dehydration and exposure despite the fact that he was close to houses and civilization.

You can hear the freeway noise from where his body washed up against a rock. Did he try to get help? Did he knock on a door and ask for water? We will never know his story.

The Sonoran Desert is an oven during the summer and dips into subfreezing temperatures in the winter. It takes a minimum of seven days to walk from the Mexican border to Tucson. If you are lucky and can find your way through the labyrinth of *arroyos* and canyons, dodging the Border Patrol agents who are in pursuit, and resisting the assault and brutality of thugs you may encounter, you might make it to a "safe house." A safe house is a secret place for sanctuary, suitable for hiding undocumented persons from the law.

Carrying enough food and water for this journey is almost impossible. Yet desperate Latinos have been making the journey for generations, and many arrive at their destinations. They live throughout the United States. There are an estimated eleven million undocumented persons living in this country. Eight million of them are Latinos.

For me desert searches are a mix of hiking in some of the most remote and beautiful country on earth and the fear that I will enter into a life-and-death situation with a migrant in serious physical trouble. As a registered nurse who has been out of the practice of emergency treatment for many years, I hope that some of the old techniques and procedures will kick in if I need them.

I carry in my backpack a blood-pressure cuff, a stethoscope, ACE bandages and a bottle of Advil. The Samaritan van is stocked with food packets, a first-aid kit, water, blankets, clothing and a GPS device in case *we* get lost.

———

We creep along at thirty mph in our aging van through the most rugged desert I have ever seen. This is a Samaritan desert search. There are four of us, and we peer intently out the windows looking for signs—a jacket hanging on a branch, a water bottle, a backpack, recent footprints in the *arroyos.* We are in wild, remote country, at least eight miles from any sign of civilization, and it is hot out here. May and June are scorchers in southern Arizona. The air conditioner in the van is cranking on "high" and we all drink nonstop from our bottles of water. I wonder how anyone can survive this kind of heat.

Our Samaritan group leader spots something up an *arroyo,* and so we stop. Armed with plastic bags to pick up *basura,* we all hike up the dry wash, calling out:

"*Somos samaritanos.*" We are Samaritans and we offer help. Food. Water. Medical aid.

Basura, the things that migrants leave behind, is like hidden treasure. I occasionally receive anti-immigration e-mails from people with pictures of trash in our desert— diapers, plastic water bottles, tattered clothing. The scenes look like a dump. On my desert searches I have never seen this kind of decimation. Instead, the *basura* has looked like clues that help me understand what kind of people are traveling across the desert.

A rosary. A plastic picture of the *Virgen de Guadalupe.* An earring, a scrap of paper with a phone number, a shoe. Sometimes an old encampment under some brush will reveal a tattered sleeping bag. Empty cans of pinto beans and little hot dogs. Plastic water bottles with Mexican labels. A zip-lock bag with medications. Once there was a beautifully embroidered cloth used to wrap tortillas. I think about the worried mother who may have created this for her son who was trying to get to *el norte.* I wonder why this piece of folk art was dropped on this lonely trail.

I'm sure there are *arroyos* and hidden encampments that are depositories for the *basura* that groups of migrants leave behind. It is probably an unsightly and stinky mess. These piles of trash are in-your-face wake-up calls to a country that is asleep and tuned out to one of the most massive migrations in human history. Subtlety does not work on Americans. Piles of garbage left behind make many angry.

I would suggest another approach. Embrace these pilgrims. Hire them. Teach them English. Learn Spanish while you're at it. Assist them in their quest for a better life in *Los Estados Unidos*. We have much to learn from each other. But first we must change the draconian and inhumane immigration policies that promote paranoia and exclusivity.

They don't work.

"Just because you don't see anyone doesn't mean they are not there," reflects Richard Calabro, our group leader on this spring day in the desert. "We will only see migrants when they are in trouble. They know we are here to help."

Migrants journey at night, when temperatures are more tolerable. They stay in the shade and rest during the heat of the day.

I think about the mountain lions and coyotes that are hidden during the day and travel at night. I look in the shadows and crevices of the *arroyos* and imagine the hidden travelers napping and quietly waiting for tolerable evening temperatures. They travel like the creatures of the desert.

I have been on many searches for migrants. Thankfully I have not encountered anyone in need of our help but have seen where they walk and where they sleep. The night before a search, I always review once again what I would do if I found someone in trouble. What are the signs of acute dehydration, hyperthermia, diabetic distress? What if someone is comatose?

Never sleeping well the night before, I wonder if I'll do the right thing. Can I handle this? What am I doing here anyway?

I must be out of my mind.

It is a felony to transport an undocumented migrant anywhere. I've thought about this a lot. Faced with another law that is morally and ethically wrong, I ponder the consequences of possibly breaking the law.

"Humanitarian Aid Is Never a Crime"—it is written in bold print on my Samaritan T-shirt. I would call 911 in an emergency, and if a response or help weren't there in ten minutes, well, I would have to test that law.

In July 2005, the Border Patrol arrested two volunteers from the humanitarian organization No More Deaths while evacuating three medically compromised individuals from the desert to a hospital in Tucson. They were later indicted on felony charges of conspiracy and aiding and abetting. In response, No More Deaths launched a support campaign called "Humanitarian Aid Is Never a Crime," prompting an overwhelming international response and eventually resulting in the dismissal of the charges against the volunteers. Providing life-giving aid as well as witnessing and responding to migrants in need is the mission of the Samaritans.

Walking up an *arroyo*, I spot a little makeshift shrine in the branch of an old mesquite tree, complete with a picture of the *Virgen de Guadalupe* and a cross. The faith of the migrants astounds me. Instead of forsaking God, they embrace their spiritual life even more. The prayers are intense. When the chips are down and all else is lost, there is that moment of truth for these pilgrims.

I imagine them visualizing their families, their children and their God. After all, what is more important? *"Vaya con Dios,"* I whisper at the little shrine and wonder what has happened to the people who passed by this sacred spot. There is the musky odor of yucca blossoms in the air, mixed with the moldy smell of an old can of beans. A torn, ragged jacket hangs on a mesquite limb. A baby shoe is half-buried in dirt. These trees have seen it all.

One of the perks about going on a desert search is the hours spent in the Samaritan van with some interesting people. One hot morning in mid-May I meet Rowland and Judy, a couple of Samaritans who spent most of their adult lives in the Philippines. They are citizens of the world and understand issues of border politics. Retired now in Green Valley, they volunteer regularly to search for lost migrants in the desert. It turns out they are also excellent birders, and so we spot a variety of species migrating north for the summer. The desert is a cornucopia now for migrating birds, as the flowers and insects provide a feast for these feathered creatures as they journey through Arizona.

―――

We head out toward Ruby Road and Sycamore Canyon, a wild and remote mountainous area with dozens of migrant trails. The Border Patrol vehicles are out in full force on this morning, and we stop and chat with several of them. Most of the agents are friendly today and share information about where we might be helpful.

"There is a lot of activity at night, but most migrants lay low during the heat of the day."

"They're all over these mountains, but you need special cameras to see them."

"You can probably spot the 'quitters' around Warsaw Gulch."

The quitters? I've never heard the migrants called quitters.

This particular Border Patrol agent, a cocky fellow with a clean-shaven head and a swagger in his gait, tells us to head up to Warsaw Gulch, where migrants may need help.

The quitters.

I get the sense that this particular agent has drunk his share of coffee this morning, as he is on a chatty roll.

We drive to Warsaw Gulch on a narrow, gravel road, bumping along at ten mph looking for anything that moves out there. All we see are more Border Patrol agents. One agent, a Mexican-American, engages us in a friendly exchange for a while as he gazes out of his truck into the wilderness, looking for people.

"I've been working with the Border Patrol for seventeen years, and this is a pretty interesting job," he tells us. We ask him for his perspective on his work. His answers are thoughtful and honest.

"My supervisors would say we need more agents, more trucks, better technology. That's not the answer. Most of the people we find out here are looking for jobs and a better life. They can't survive in Mexico. I say that Mexico needs to get its act together so people don't need to migrate."

He went on to say that the "dope runners" need to be

stopped, but they are not the people he sees or hears about today when he gazes through his binoculars or listens on his two-way radio for reports from others.

"The people I see are desperate," he continues. "They can't survive in Mexico, because of the economy and the violence connected with the drug cartels."

He spoke with nostalgia about the wonderful trips he used to take to Chihuahua, Mexico, with his family as a boy.

"There is no way I will travel in Mexico now. There are too many hot spots that are controlled by the cartels." We all agree that the immigration policies of the United States need to change and that Mexico and our own country must try to work together. I feel like we are on the same page with this fellow. He thanks us for the work we do.

On another desert search, I traveled with Mike Casey, a seasoned aid worker who lived and worked for many years in Ethiopia. On this particular day we stop in Ruby, a deserted mining town with a population of one, the caretaker. The town is remote but with many vacant houses and buildings still standing. It is a great place to poke around and imagine what life was like 150 years ago when silver, gold and lead were pulled out of these hills.

The caretaker lives in an RV and has also set up housekeeping in one of the crumbling houses. The setting is rugged and rocky, with a nearby reservoir pond full of trout and bass. It is a lonely life, but our caretaker friend seems to be handling it well. His dog, Karli, keeps him company.

"Here, try some of my homemade jerky," he says and offers us some spicy dried beef he has just made with his new food drier. It is chewy and delicious, perfect for a long day's hike in the surrounding hills. He frequently sees migrants coming through Ruby and helps them if they need it. He tells us that most want to continue on even though he warns them of the treacherous landscape, the heat, the lack of water and the armed patrols who search for them.

Our caretaker friend has recently gotten his computer and printer hooked up to the outside world, and he is hungry to discuss the affairs of Arizona and national politics. We speak of war, of peace, and the migration of people crossing the desert to reach their families and a new life.

After visiting with this affable fellow for a while, we head toward Arivaca, another Arizona town known for its quirky ways, aging hippies and strongly opinionated residents. It is time for lunch at Virginia's, a taco stand that dishes out amazing Mexican cuisine under a shady sycamore tree. We are ready for Virginia's famous burritos, her salsa and a watermelon smoothie.

A couple of locals sit nearby, and the familiar smell of Arivaca's most famous herb wafts over to our table. It feels like the 1960s. The arrival of the food provides the perfect postlude to a day in the desert. Maybe it is a contact high from the herbal smoke, but my guess is that Virginia is just a damn good cook.

Sometime in the middle of lunch a woman sits down at our table and begins to tell us her story. She is from Cleveland and has lived in Arivaca for six years. A former home-health caretaker for an elderly gentleman who has recently died, she is in a state of transition. She speaks about the contrasts between Cleveland and Arivaca and thinks she will probably stay. The magic and quirkiness of Arivaca have enveloped this woman. She likes it here.

And she likes us, too. Cleveland lady tells us with commitment and passion that there is only one thing to do when she sees a migrant passing through Arivaca: Give him water, food and help if he needs it. There is no question in her mind that this is the only answer to the migrant issue.

I love ending a day in the desert with this kind of affirmation from a stranger.

Unsolicited, too.

THE DARK SIDE

Recently the newspaper headlines reported a massacre of forty-nine people found dumped along a major highway outside Monterrey, Mexico. The bodies were without limbs and had been decapitated. This makes it impossible to identify the bodies—no fingerprints, no heads, just the grisly work of the Zeta drug cartel. The war for territory and drug trafficking goes on unabated. The Zetas are entangled in a horrific irrational conflict with the Sinaloa cartel over power and money. The kingpins of these two groups are worth billions.

When I read of carnage like this I think to myself, "Let them kill each other off. The world will be a better place without the insanity of the warring drug cartels."

But, of course, we do not know who these forty-nine victims lying along the highway are. Some say they were migrants heading north to the border. They may have been innocent people heading to *el norte* for jobs and economic survival. Others claim they are drug runners. We may never know the truth behind this massacre.

I cannot forget that the reason the cartels have become such a powerful festering unpredictable force is that the market for illicit drugs in the United States is insatiable. America is the buyer, no matter the cost. Mexico has the product and no price is too high. We are in this together. The problems of Mexico are binational. There would not be this kind of irrational killing if Americans didn't demand their recreational highs. And the pockets of the drug lords are not lined with yen or euros. They are lined with U.S. dollars.

So this kind of news gives me pause as I walk with my Samaritan comrades to *el comedor.* Nogales is a major port of entry for illicit drugs, most entering the United States via huge semitrucks that carry produce from Mexico and Central America. I confess that I look around carefully at some of the parked pickups on the one-mile walk to the *comedor.* Who are these guys who seem to stay parked in their trucks each week? They are always on a cell phone. Are these the good guys? Or the bad guys?

There is a code of conduct that presents a startling change of mood and behavior when walking on the U.S. side of the border and then crossing over to the Mexican side. On the U.S. side there is no eye contact with officials or pedestrians I pass on the path to the border. Especially if the pedestrian is a gringo. There are many persons in uniform milling around, and all are armed. I see dark blue uniforms, green uniforms, gray uniforms, all representing some department of Homeland Security.

The Samaritans march along quietly, occasionally taking a photo of the construction of the wall. Occasionally we are told, "No photos! This is a secure area!"

One time the director of a local American nonprofit

organization was walking toward the border port of entry, not sure which path was the correct one. The signs were made of flimsy pieces of cardboard. Nothing looked very official. He was walking on the U.S. side, and after several yards, four ICE agents with rifles at the ready surrounded him and sharply commanded him to stop and state his business.

"Where are you going? What do you think you're doing?" a Border Patrol agent barked loudly.

The director expressed his genuine confusion about where he should be walking, as there were no clear signs to guide him. The agents pointed him in the right direction. Startled during the encounter and not accustomed to the weaponry and admonishments when innocently taking a wrong path, the director quickly changed his course and found the correct passage. The incident made a deep impression on him. The border is a war zone.

As soon as the Samaritans cross into Mexico, the Latino pedestrians and peddlers and newspaper boys and ice cream vendors all give a shout-out to our little group. *"Buenos días! Hola! Cómo estás?"* is heard again and again. There are high-fives. Truck drivers waiting in line honk their horns and wave. Samaritans have a good reputation on the other side of the fence. Those red baseball hats with *Samaritans* written on them and the official Samaritan T-shirts are recognized everywhere. When strangers call out to you in greeting, it is a great feeling. Ironically, I feel safer as soon as I cross the line into Mexico. Fewer guns, more smiles.

Those visuals in the newspapers of bodies alongside the road fade in my mind. Monterrey is a long distance from

Nogales. And besides, who would harm a shelter run by Jesuits and the Sisters of the Eucharist?

But I do keep my head up. This ain't Kansas, Toto. Mexico has many dangerous pockets where violence can erupt unexpectedly.

I tend to romanticize the migrants and the street peddlers. Taken at face value, the street people are engaging and friendly and seem to enjoy the interaction. I meet their families and learn of their struggles. Many of the street peddlers are migrants who have decided to stay in Nogales and survive as best they can, selling ice cream, trinkets and newspapers.

But I am wary, too. I am a guest in Mexico and cross the border once or twice a week. I realize that I am scratching the surface of day-to-day life in this border town and am a privileged visitor.

~~~~

And so it is on one particular day that our Samaritan group approaches the *comedor* and there are several Mexican police cars parked in front. This has never happened before.

"Why are you here? You were not supposed to come today!" Father Francisco excitedly greets us, meeting us at the entrance of *el comedor.* An incident occurred yesterday at the shelter, but the Samaritans did not get the message via e-mail or telephone. I hear four versions of the incident from KBI staff, but the one that sounds most plausible comes from Francisco.

Two male migrants came running to the *comedor* yesterday, followed closely by a pickup truck with a couple of men. The migrants sought sanctuary inside the shelter, and the men in the pickup shouted at them and tried to enter themselves. Father Ed McFadden, one of the priests at the shelter, stepped outside to see what the commotion was about. Francisco was close behind. The two men in the truck spoke with Father Ed in a threatening manner, poking their fingers into his chest and grasping his shirt. They wanted the two migrants inside.

Someone inside the *comedor* called the police and they were there within minutes. By this time the two running migrants had escaped out the back somehow, and Francisco said that the police had a conversation with the men in the pickup truck. Then the men in the pickup drove away. The police promised to watch the *comedor* and make their armed presence felt for a few days.

Francisco is shaky when describing this incident. It is the first time he has been confronted by men he considers dangerous and possibly armed. As a novice Jesuit for the past nine months, he has seen a lot. But never this kind of confrontation. No one saw a gun, but both Francisco and Father Ed believed that the men were armed. The one hundred or more migrants inside the shelter having breakfast were terrified, according to Francisco.

Father Sean Carroll, the KBI director, immediately called for a moratorium on visits from volunteer groups until the situation was sorted out. Two weeks went by and the Samaritans returned to do their regular relief work each Tuesday. There have been no further incidents.

Despair.

So this is Mexico. A land of sporadic lawlessness and violence and love and joy and generosity. I have found a place
to go each week where love and generosity of spirit reign.
But you never know when someone will wreak havoc. It can
happen anywhere—even in an upscale Safeway parking lot
in Tucson.

The thought never leaves me.

An article in *The New York Times*[4] speaks of the numbing
of the people of Mexico.

A massacre at a shopping mall? Oh well, we will avoid
that area and shop for items out of sight of the mayhem.
Hopefully they will clean up the mess before we are fin-
ished with our errands.

Mass graves found outside of the city? We will not drive

our cars near that area and will keep our children from reading the newspapers today.

Mexicans say they have no choice but to go on with their lives. Fifty-thousand killed in Mexico since 2006? Probably more as the mass graves are discovered. Sadly, we are all getting used to the bloodshed.

But it's not just Mexico. I am getting used to the numbers killed in Iraq and Afghanistan. The massacres in our own shopping malls, schools, theaters and military bases leave me numb. How can we bemoan the wars and violence in other countries when our own country is always on the brink of some crisis?

When there is carnage in the world, I read about it, take a deep breath and move on. And pray I don't get caught up in the crossfire. It is a sort of anesthesia. It is a dream world. As long as the bloodshed is over there, wherever over there is, and as long as my children are not in the middle of it all, I sleep well.

I welcome the numbness.

OPERATION STREAMLINE

One bright spring day in Tucson, I had my day in court. I witnessed Operation Streamline, the court system that speeds up due process for the thousands of immigrants who have entered the United States illegally. Operation Streamline first began back in 2005 during George W. Bush's Presidency. Any American can sit in the courtroom in Tucson and observe what happens to approximately seventy undocumented migrants every day, Monday through Friday. It is an eye-opener.

~~~

The courtroom is large. The benches look like church pews. The air-conditioning unit gives the room a stagnant, dead chill. As I enter the space, I notice that the left side of the room is filled with people with brown faces, all seated on the hard benches; on the right side are small groups of predominantly white men in uniform milling about. Seventy migrants sit quietly and stoically on those benches. All are Latino. Dressed in T-shirts and dusty jeans, they look like they have been in the desert for days. Their belts and shoelaces have been removed. There are two female migrants who sit separately from the men. All are in shackles—their hands attached to a chain around their waist, feet manacled at the ankles.

I watch as a migrant tries to drink water from a paper cup. It is impossible to drink without bending at the waist and precariously ingesting the water against gravity. The water spills down the young man's T-shirt as he tries to take a sip. When they stand, some of them have difficulty keeping their pants up without a belt. I am embarrassed to watch this and quickly look away.

All eyes are on our group of six as we enter the courtroom and are told where to sit, which is on the far right side of the room, away from the migrants. The looks from the captives are beseeching, searching, as if we might be family or a friend. There are a few smiles from the migrants. I smile back, tentatively, not quite knowing how to behave in this setting. A few of the men look like people I have seen at the *comedor*.

One fellow has on baggy "skater" shorts and a silky soccer T-shirt. He looks like a California dude raised on McDonald's hamburgers and is heavier and larger than any other migrant. He grins at our group and gives us a little wave.

The men in uniform on the right side of the room are Border Patrol officers and U.S. marshals. On this side of the courtroom the atmosphere is one of laughing, joking, a feeling of business as usual and easy camaraderie. Several are playing with their iPhones and Internet devices.

On the left there is silence as the migrant defendants stare into their laps or vacantly straight ahead. I notice that one of the lawyers and a Border Patrol officer are also Latino, and it occurs to me that they are the only Hispanics in the room who are not in shackles. The majority of migrants look young, in their teens, twenties or early thirties.

All have earphones—translation instruments so they can understand the court proceedings, which are in English. They each have a federal public defender who has spent the morning with his assigned cases—usually about six cases per lawyer.

An attorney friend who works one day a week doing Operation Streamline cases has explained to our group the mechanics and protocol of this courtroom experience.

"These are the nicest people that I defend. Their only crime is crossing the border to find work," he tells us. My friend is supportive of the migrants' plight and gives me insight into the proceedings of this streamlined form of justice. He doesn't approve of the cookie-cutter approach to

Streamline and is as responsive and informative to the migrants as he can be. It is a tough job.

I am impressed with all the attorneys that day. They take their jobs seriously and do their best to be fair and just and humane with their clients.

When the judge enters, we all stand. The judge is a woman. As she takes roll call with each migrant, she pronounces every name correctly in Spanish. She is patient and empathetic with each person. Her demeanor and her caring, coupled with her objectivity as a judge, are inspiring. I wonder what she thinks of this whole judicial encounter.

One fellow does not know his birth date, and she speaks with him about his best guess regarding his age. He decides he is "maybe nineteen." Another fellow states his birthplace as Guatemala when it is actually Chiapas, Mexico. It turns out that Chiapas was part of Guatemala 180 years ago and was annexed by Mexico. The man's family has never accepted the change.

This business of borders exists far beyond our own.

The migrants are called to the bench in groups of six. Their bony frames are hunched over from the weight of the leg irons and manacles. The clanging of the metal irons and the shuffling to the front of the room is a sight I will never forget. I think about drawings in history books of African slaves in this country two hundred years ago.

Each migrant is asked, "Are you a citizen of Mexico (or Guatemala, El Salvador, Honduras), and did you enter into the U.S. illegally?"

"*Sí.*"

"Are you being forced to plead guilty?"

"*No*"

"Have you spent time discussing your situation with your lawyer?"

"*Sí.*"

After several more questions, the judge asks, "How do you plead?"

"*Culpable*" or "Guilty," the migrants say one by one.

The California skater dude says, "Guilty," and tells the judge that he was visiting extended family in Mexico and was trying to get back home to Tucson when he was detained in Nogales. He speaks perfect English. He looks like a high school kid.

Each migrant is given the opportunity to speak. All know that by pleading guilty, they will get back to Mexico more quickly. Their lawyers have advised them well. The migrants have the right to a trial by jury if they wish to plead not guilty, but this means weeks in a prison or a detention center awaiting trial and the probability that they will be deported anyway.

Not much of a choice.

If this is a first-time offender, the sentence is fifteen to thirty days, with time served counted as part of the sentence. If the migrant has other charges (a theft or driving without a license, for example), the sentence is thirty to 180 days, but if the plea is "guilty," the lesser offense is what is considered when a judgment is made. Sometimes the sentencing seems arbitrary, but it appears that the judge has more information about each migrant than is evident to those of us in the gallery.

The question that occurs to me is, does this work? Does this conveyor-belt approach to justice deter illegal entry into the United States?

The newspapers and other media tell me that the numbers of migrants are down. The Border Patrol apprehended a thousand migrants a day along the Arizona border in 2012 and seemed to cherry-pick seventy of them for Operation Streamline. The rest were quickly deported into Nogales, the busiest exit point in the state.[5]

Most of the migrants I see in Nogales tell me that what deters them from crossing are poor economic conditions in the United States and the harsh dangers of the desert journey. And even these deterrents do not dissuade many from seeking to reunite with families and loved ones. They will cross regardless of Operation Streamline or incarceration. One young migrant told me that even if he is caught and put in a detention center, it is "better than my village in Honduras."

And what about the cost? As I remain in the air-conditioned chambers of the federal courthouse in Tucson, sitting on hard Presbyterian benches watching judgments come down from on high (the judge *is* up on a platform), I wonder about the dollars spent on Operation Streamline. It is hard to pin down an accurate monetary figure. As usual, there is no easy answer.

First there is Homeland Security, which includes the Border Patrol and ICE. In 2003 the budget was $9.1 billion. The budget in 2010 was $17.2 billion.[6] Then there's the wall at the U.S.-Mexican border, a $42 billion project and growing.[7] The length of the U.S.-Mexican border is 1,969 miles; the length of the border fence is 650 miles. Add to this the incarceration facilities and the growing private prison system that is headed by the Corrections Corporation of America (CCA).

The privatization of the prison system is a controversial topic. A monthly check of $13 million is paid to CCA by the U.S. marshal in Arizona. The private prison system is Arizona's growth industry. If you have a penchant for emotional detachment and disengagement from people and like to wield some power, there are jobs for you with CCA.[8]

The courts, the prisons and the law enforcement agencies all prosper. The prisons make money if the cells are full. Ergo, more migrant detainees mean more profits for CCA.

And the taxpayers foot the bill.

In my opinion, the biggest cost is the humanitarian one: criminalizing people who have not committed a crime. Watching seventy people in chains and manacles shuffling through the courtroom with the American flag in full display is unnerving. Watching this spectacle and knowing that their crime is crossing the U.S. border looking for work touches me at a visceral level. This is what my own ancestors did when they crossed the pond just three or four generations ago. We are criminalizing people who want to work.

Most of the people I see in that courtroom are going to make it, either here or back in their country of origin. This is their odyssey, not unlike Homer's tale. There are monsters to slay, sirens that offer temptations, cyclopes to tackle and a journey of danger and daring. The myth of *The Odyssey* has come to life a few miles from my home. The migrants in this courtroom may leave the room shuffling in chains with their heads down, but like Odysseus, they will not give up.

As I watch one of the migrants leave the courtroom in chains, he tries to cross himself as he whispers a prayer. His chains restrict his movement. This simple eloquent gesture stays with me the rest of the day.

So here is what I take away from this profound day in court. If there is a chance for a better life, be it here or somewhere else, these people in chains are going to take it. And probably succeed.

I really believe that.

Shura and her vision of peace.

CHAPTER THREE

Summer

Summer in the Sonoran Desert is like the dead of winter in northern climes. Extreme temperatures. Naps in the afternoon. People on the border stay indoors in their air-conditioned offices and homes. Retired folks like me hibernate during the day. We work on projects that have been put off throughout the year—organizing photos for albums, starting a quilt for a new grandchild, catching up on all those *New Yorker* magazines. It is simply too hot to be outside during the day.

The only hospitable time is early in the morning and in the shadows of evening. The desert is merciful at night and cools dramatically. Mornings are the best times to be out in the yard working in the garden. We drink our morning coffee at five and watch the birds arrive at the feeders.

May and June are the hottest months of the year. July brings the monsoon rain that transforms the parched desert into a lush green jungle of flowering bushes and grasses.

Just when you thought the desert was in the throes of death, a wellspring of rain saturates the landscape.

But there is always an edge to the season's changes. The rains are never gentle. They pour from the heavens with a vengeance. Streets flood, *arroyos* gush, cars are swept away in road gullies and underpasses. There is always some treachery behind the blessings of the rain. Almost every summer, a child will be playing in an arroyo and a monsoon flash flood will sweep the little one away. There are pileups on the freeways as drivers struggle to see through the torrents of water on the windshield.

Once on a flight home from Oregon, my plane was diverted into Mexico and arrived a half-hour late in Tucson because of the monsoon winds buffeting the aircraft, making a safe landing impossible. Lightning was flashing on both sides of the plane, and the passengers were sitting quietly wondering how this was going to play out. When we finally landed in Tucson, the sun was shining and the storm had passed.

During a monsoon storm, I think about the migrants traveling through the desert and wonder how they survive. Did they find a cave or shelter? Were they caught in a wall of water in a narrow canyon? The scorched earth welcomes the downpour, but what of the pilgrims trapped in the middle of the desert with no place to hide from the elements?

BURN MAN

On a sweltering day in June, there is a small group in front of the *comedor* just hanging around, sitting on the curb, never entering the sanctuary of the shelter. The old-timers whisper that these are *coyotes*, possibly members of the drug cartels, maybe some local peddlers and homeless people doing their best to survive in Nogales. They are a mixed bag of poor people hoping for a pair of socks from the Samaritans or perhaps a baseball cap to protect them from the incessant sun.

One fellow in particular has captured my interest during the past weeks. He wears a filthy brown hoodie when the temperature is a hundred degrees or more and usually hits up the Samaritans for cigarettes and a Coke. A cloud of flies often follows this fellow, sort of like Pigpen, the character in the comic strip *Peanuts*.

Fellow Samaritan Ricardo, always a soft touch, usually takes this person across the street to a small mini-market and buys him something to eat and a pack of cigarettes. As it turns out, our wandering flycatcher is named Sergio, and he is a homeless vagrant who often sleeps in the cemetery. He is not allowed inside the *comedor*, because on occasion he has become disruptive. And he is not officially a migrant but a Mexican citizen who is homeless. The KBI mission is to serve the migrant population that is on the move, and Sergio lives on the streets of Nogales.

"Hey, Peg, come over here!" a Samaritan colleague, Harry, calls to me, and I hurry over to the first-aid station.

Sergio has staggered in and Nurse Norma is stripping off his shirt. His back is covered with second- and third-degree burns. Infection is rampant. I can smell the foul septic odors from the door. The man howls in pain as Norma and her aide, Jacobo, clean his wounds. A couple of people hold Sergio down as Norma does her best to remove the dead tissue and infected areas.

I ask what has happened, and Jacobo answers tentatively, "It's complicated."

It seems that a group of bullies poured battery acid on this helpless soul several nights ago, and Sergio has come begging for help today. He has suffered silently for days. Of course, I thought the man should be hospitalized, but for reasons I still don't understand, this didn't happen. But with Norma's careful and gentle ministrations, with days and weeks of cleansing this man's scorched back, Sergio slowly recovers.

Three or more times a week, Sergio shows up at the first-aid station for the torture of having his wounds cleaned, which is always done without pain medication or anesthesia. I leave a small bottle of Advil with Norma, which is like medicating with orange juice for major surgery. Each time he cries out in pain, and several aides hold him while Norma works on his back. It is a horror show, but both Norma and Sergio are committed to the task.

For many months Sergio waits for the Samaritans to arrive at *el comedor*. He always turns his back to us, usually in the middle of the street, and raises his ragged shirt to show how his back is healing. And asks for cigarettes and a Coke.

It becomes apparent that Sergio is a disabled person, both mentally and physically. He is an outcast on the streets of Nogales. Communication is limited. His needs are simple: He wants his nicotine and a hit of caffeine. Things do go better with Coke.

Every Tuesday I see Sister Rosalba come out to the curb in front of the *comedor* carrying a plate piled high with rice and beans and chicken for Sergio. He sits on the sidewalk with trucks and taxis whizzing by and he eats. And he drinks down a big glass of milk.

And then, of course, he asks for those cigarettes and the requisite Coke.

I look forward to seeing Sergio each week. He has a face of innocence—a face of trust. He looks fourteen. He looks forty.

A couple of times I try to talk him into a clean shirt and jacket. He refuses. Wrong color. He prefers brown. Nothing else will do. He means no harm to anyone.

Sergio is one of those people who make me ponder how I was born into a life of plenty and how he was born into a life of figuring out how to stay alive day after day. I know life isn't fair, but his predicament seems so totally unjust and unnecessary. And yet there is a serenity about this guy. He carries a small cardboard suitcase around with his worldly possessions—a filthy blanket, some packs of cigarettes and not much else.

The miracle of this sad little tale is that Sergio's back healed quite nicely. Scarring, yes, and pain when he stretches, he tells us. But he is back wandering the streets of Nogales with his little cardboard suitcase. He smiles and waves to us each week and always lifts his shirt to show us his back. And hits up fellow Samaritan Ricardo for cigarettes and a Coke.

THE MAN FROM OAXACA

As July approaches, the famed "dry heat" of Arizona is

gone. The humidity is high and we sweat in the intense temperatures, searching the heavens each day for signs of a
storm. Ballooning thunderhead clouds swell each afternoon, and we watch as sheets of moisture fall from the sky
but never reach the earth. The rains evaporate before touching the parched desert. It is maddening.

There is an awareness of air. It feels like you are stepping
into an oven. You feel the hotness on your skin. You feel the
heat as you inhale. Breathing deeply is painful. The lungs
feel singed.

This is the time when the desert is deadliest. Migrants
from the tropics of southern Mexico and Central America
have no idea what kind of inferno awaits them when they
arrive at the border. When a body is discovered, often it has
been in the desert for months, even years. Or sometimes
just a day. It is a sobering and grisly fact of life when hiking
in Arizona. You may come across a body. The thought flick-
ers in the back of my mind, always.

When I did the rim-to-rim hike across the Grand Canyon several years ago, I learned that your feet are your most
important tool. If you develop severe blisters or a sprain,
that's it—the show is over.

Each night our trekking guide would inspect our feet
and make recommendations. Any hot spots (reddened
areas) were quickly treated with antibiotic ointment and
duct tape. Yes, duct tape. Duct tape won't slip off as easily
in hot desert climates. Forget moleskin and most other blis-
ter remedies—the high temperatures of the desert quickly
disintegrate wraps and tapes inside shoes. Duct tape to the
rescue. It stays in place and cushions your feet. It keeps the

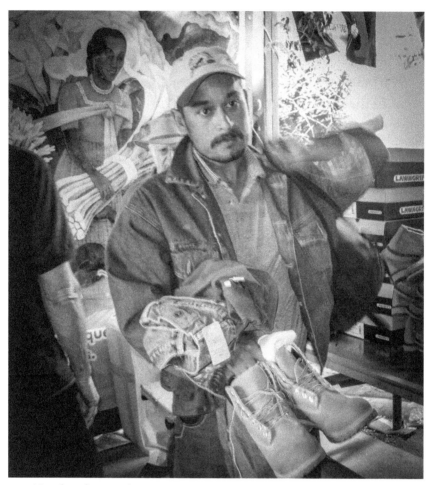

New shoes for a new day.

universe from unraveling. Always hike with a roll of duct tape in your backpack.

Working at the small first-aid station near the *comedor,* I saw blistered feet like I have never seen in my life. Hiking the Sonoran Desert in ill-fitting shoes will break down your feet in a very short time. My visits to the little first-aid

station were mostly spent on the hard concrete floor on my
bony knees washing the feet of exhausted men and women
who had been hiking the desert trying to get to Tucson or
Ajo or to a waiting van on some isolated road.

In the spring of 2011, the Mexican first-aid station was a
small cinder-block building with a sink that did not produce water and a toilet that did not flush. In a word, this was
a primitive setup. Water for washing wounds was carried in
buckets from the *comedor* across the street. The sloshing
buckets were set on Bunsen burners to warm. It felt like
Africa or Afghanistan. Some mornings it was bone-chill-
ingly cold, but by noon it was sweltering in this tiny building. A small fan was clickety-clacking, trying to move the
stifling air. I dreamed of rain and cool breezes as I waited
for the patients to show up.

More than once I wondered what the hell I was doing
there.

───

A fellow limps into the clinic looking hot, tired and tattered. He appears to be twenty years old, tops. The Border
Patrol picked him up just outside Tijuana and brought him
to Nogales, Sonora, for reasons I don't understand. Later I
learn that migrants are often deported many miles from
their original port-of-entry location in order to discourage
future crossings.

There are cactus puncture wounds, a bad ankle sprain
and two blistered feet with the skin torn off. He speaks perfect English and tells me he is heading to Wichita, Kansas,
where he grew up.

Kansas?

It turns out he had been in Kansas since he was a baby but after high school went back to Oaxaca to see relatives. There he fell in love and got married and now has a two-year-old daughter. Pulling a wrinkled photo of a baby from his jeans pocket, he gets choked up.

Then he abruptly asks me, "How about them Packers? Do you know how the Kansas City Chiefs are doing? What do you think of the Arizona Diamondbacks?"

My Oaxaca friend is a sports nut. And he is trying to ease my discomfort as I kneel on the hard floor trying to wash his feet. We eye each other self-consciously.

"What were you going to do in Wichita?" I ask him. "Why did you leave your wife and baby in Oaxaca?"

"I'm a fabulous Mexican tile-setter," he tells me. He has a good job with a construction company in Wichita. "Gringos love what I do with bathrooms and kitchens." Making five times the salary he would earn in Oaxaca, he decided it was worth the risk to try to cross the border and return to Wichita. He planned to stay for six months, send money to his wife and then come home to Oaxaca and his family.

"Why didn't you ever apply for citizenship when you were in Kansas?" I ask him.

He shrugs and tells me he didn't know he was undocumented until he was sixteen years old.

"I didn't think it was that big of a deal," he tells me. He says he was always able to cross back and forth in the past to see family in Mexico.

He winces as I soak his feet in warm water and Epsom salts in the little plastic tubs.

My patient is quietly thinking. I gingerly pick away the dead skin from his feet with some sterile forceps I find in a drawer. I focus on the job at hand, picking away at his swollen feet; he watches me work, flinching in pain when I hit a tender spot. Sweat drips down my nose as my migrant friend also sweats.

Finally he says, "I'm not going to try this again. It is tough for me in Oaxaca, but there are too many cops now looking for us in the U.S."

My Samaritan colleagues and I chip in and buy this fellow a bus ticket back to Oaxaca and give him money for food. He chokes up again and asks if I watched the Super Bowl last winter.

"How about them Packers?" he repeats.

I feel like I am talking with a kid from L.A. who wants to watch a football game today with his American friends.

"I'd like to see your tile work sometime."

He grins and tells me to look him up in Oaxaca.

Washing someone's feet while kneeling on a concrete floor in the heat and humidity of a monsoon day in July is a humbling experience. Especially when the patient is an exhausted migrant who has been shuffled around by Border Patrol and immigration agents. As I slowly try to remove the dead skin and dirt from a lineup of migrants with their feet in plastic tubs, many cross themselves.

"*Gracias,*" they whisper to me.

They try not to wince. I try not to keel over on the concrete, my face shiny with sweat. It is quite a tableau—my white hair and knobby knees and their winces and tears and prayers.

Never as a registered nurse in the United States have I had this experience. Kneeling before a suffering migrant, gently trying to wash the miles of dust and dirt from mutilated, bloody feet, is an act of overwhelming emotion.

It all took me by surprise. It was at once biblical, physically painful for me (my knees, my back) and excruciating for my pilgrim patient. It is an act of love; it is an act of pain.

The migrants look at times fearful, amazed and somewhat incredulous. An American lady old enough to be their grandmother is washing their feet. It is a first for them. It is a first for me. We muddle through it together. After I have applied the antibiotic ointment and dressed the feet, they hobble out into the sun.

I know their journey will be halted for a time in order for their feet to heal. There is no way they can hike anywhere in the next few days. The journey has temporarily stalled here in Nogales. The future will have to wait. If you can't walk, you don't migrate.

CHICAGO ROOTS

I first noticed Victor when he was leaving *el comedor* after breakfast. He shook my hand and thanked me profusely for the wonderful meal and the welcoming, kind people. Speaking a mixture of English and Spanish, he was not quite sure what language worked best when speaking to me. He looked trendy and well groomed, with a nicely trimmed goatee and a shaved head, complete with an earring stud in his left ear. Not your usual migrant fashion statement. His T-shirt had a U.S. Marine slogan on it. I asked in Spanish where he was from, and he answered in perfect English that he was from Chicago.

Chicago, eh? My hometown.

I ask what part of Chicago (north side) and how long he's lived there (fifteen years). He points to a small woman who is going through the table of women's clothes and tells me that this is his wife, Edwina. So like all Chicagoans, we chat about the hometown.

Does he like the Cubs or the White Sox? Where did he go to school? It turns out that he is from a much fancier part of Chicago than I am. Both Edwina and Victor went to Catholic-academy high schools and lived near the beaches of Lake Michigan. I grew up on the south side, a working-class Irish-Catholic neighborhood. Edwina, or "Eddie" as she prefers, is the manager of a McDonald's hamburger franchise. Victor is a chef and specializes in Greek and Italian cooking. We discuss the nuances of dolmas, a Greek delicacy, and the sauces of Northern Italy. He knows how to make several kinds of gnocchi.

And here they are at *el comedor* in search of a change of clothes and a good meal.

They are on their way to Caborca, a small village near the Sea of Cortez in Mexico. Victor's parents live in Caborca, and he is needed at home to help with their care as they get older. They have three children, who are now in Caborca with the grandparents. Victor and Eddie are undocumented workers and have tried many times to obtain work visas, but the bureaucracy and path to being a legal worker is Byzantine and expensive.

They are tired of feeling hunted and living in constant

fear of deportation. They know the Sonoran Desert is a death trap, and besides, their children could never make the journey with them. So they are leaving the United States legally, and they both emphasize this to me several times. They are not being deported.

"We cannot stay in the U.S. and live in fear all the time. We may be deported and the kids will be left behind." All three children are U.S. citizens.

"I have not been deported to Mexico," Victor repeats. "We are leaving voluntarily. We were living well in Chicago, but I cannot work and worry all the time about getting picked up by ICE."

The kids are not happy with this decision. They miss their hamburgers and pizzas and school in Chicago. Nagging their parents about going back to Chicago, they mourn the pets and toys and friends they left behind. Eddie is concerned about their education. Victor feels guilty and ambivalent about leaving their life and their jobs.

"They only go to school four hours in Mexico! That is not enough," both parents complain to me. We talk about homeschooling. They are on top of it and have already explored online homeschooling curricula. Victor tells me he wants to return to Chicago "the right way." He wants work visas for both himself and Eddie and wants to pursue the path to U.S. citizenship. At this point it is a ten-year wait, minimum.

Vincent and Edwina are here at the *comedor* with no money, few clothes and a lot of hope. Their belongings have been stolen during their days in Nogales, and both are frightened and eager to leave. Vincent looks embarrassed. He has never had to ask for help, but desperate times call for courage.

This couple needs money for a bus ticket to Caborca, and the Samaritans empty their pockets and miraculously come up with enough. We give them some extra money for food on the journey.

There are some interesting moments in this encounter at the bus station. It almost feels like Victor and Eddie are waiting for some kind of hitch from us. What do we want from them? Are we going to begin a long-winded religious pitch? Do we expect some sort of favor from them?

When we part ways, them with their bus ticket in hand and us with big goofy smiles on our faces, Victor reaches into his pocket and gives me a one-peso coin. He confesses with some chagrin that this is his last coin. Worth about twelve cents.

"When you look at this coin, think about us, OK?" he says. "And come and visit us in Caborca sometime."

Ricardo tells them that he rides his motorcycle down to Caborca quite often, and now he'll have someone to visit. There are hugs and murmurs of *"Vaya con Dios"* all around.

Arriving home that evening, I place the coin on a little altar along with some other memorabilia and gifts from migrants. I have a very good feeling about this family. I can visualize Victor opening up a four-star Greek/Italian/Mexican restaurant someday high on a cliff with a drop-dead view of the sea.

A DAY TO REMEMBER

On a July day, my Samaritan friend Ricardo and I are in the

small first-aid station. It is monsoon season and the humidity and temperature are soaring.

Things are slow at the clinic. We are making little packets that include a toothbrush, toothpaste, soap and a disposable razor for the migrants to use when they arrive here after days of grime and sweat in the desert. Today there is plenty of sweat right here in this little cell block of a clinic. It is a hundred degrees and 80 percent humidity, and mushrooming thunderclouds promise a downpour in the afternoon if we are lucky. The air smells of rotting garbage outside the small building and disinfectant inside the steamy waiting room.

—*m*—

Two guys walk in, each holding the other up. They have been shot. One fellow shows us his thigh. The bullet has passed through his leg. The fact that it didn't hit his femoral artery is grace from above. The other guy still has a bullet in his buttocks, and inexplicably he seems the stronger of the two. The leg-wound victim is septic: he is glassy-eyed, delirious, feverish and a bit out of his head with pain. He was shot eight days ago on a train in Sinaloa. The train is known as "*la bestia*," (the beast), and many migrants lose limbs and sometimes their lives traveling on this train to Nogales.

The two men are from Honduras and are trying to get to Oregon. The harvest of apples, pears and peaches is the lure to *el norte*. They plan to harvest the fruit of the Pacific Northwest in Oregon and Washington.

Bandits assaulted the men and stole their meager belongings.

We have all seen the old western movies where the cowboy bites down on a stick and the cranky surgeon wields his scalpel after taking a swig of whiskey. The Mexican nurse, Norma, and I are thrust into this scenario with no access to pain medication and no way to adequately clean this man's infected wound. Last seen by a doctor in Sinaloa, our patient was given an antibiotic and developed a severe allergic reaction. So he has gone untreated for eight days.

His leg is red and swollen to twice the normal size. My nurse colleague pours hydrogen peroxide on the wound and we try to squeeze the purulent infection out of the open puncture caused by the bullet. Our patient screams in pain. My colleagues try to control him and hold him while we do our best to cleanse this wound. It is a nightmare. A living nightmare. We give him a T-shirt to bite on.

A thought crosses my mind: I have no business being here; I don't know how to care for this battered soul. In fact, I feel a bit faint, which is no way for a nurse to feel.

"He must get to a hospital or he won't make it," I say out loud to whoever is listening.

Nurse Norma shrugs. "He'll be OK. And if not …" She shrugs again. Norma has seen so much more than I have.

We cannot get him into the Nogales hospital, because he is not a Mexican national. He is from Honduras, and he has no money. So Ricardo suggests walking to a pharmacy and seeing if we can get an antibiotic and some strong drugs for pain. After all, it's Mexico. We don't need a prescription for everything, right? We step outside the clinic into the oven of July.

I fumble in my backpack for sunglasses, a water bottle and a hat. The streets are deserted; it is high noon, and no

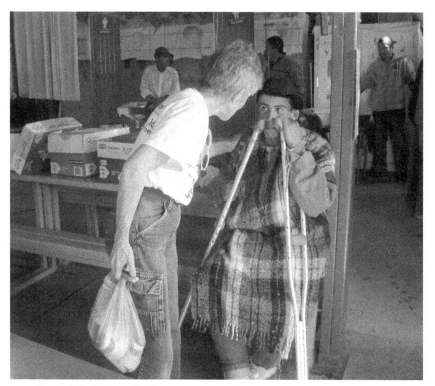

Counsel for the days ahead.

one takes a stroll in July with triple-digit temperatures. Struggling to keep up with Ricardo's pace, I push myself as best I can. We have a mile of walking through the neighborhoods of Nogales before we find a pharmacy where the owner speaks a little English. Pooling our resources of fourteen dollars, we buy a potent antibiotic and a strong narcotic for pain.

Thank you, God. There are angels everywhere. We hurry back to the clinic, where the migrant with the leg wound is sprawled on the curb waiting for us. He looks bad. Yellow, in fact. A film is over his eyes.

"Take this pill threes times a day and this one twice a

day," I say, hoping our wounded friend can understand my Spanish. Ricardo writes it all down on the back of a paper bag. I pour a couple of pills into the man's hand and give him some bottled water to wash it down.

The desperately ill migrant smiles weakly, crosses himself and thanks us. His friend, the guy with the bullet in the buttocks, assures us he'll take care of him.

But what about you? What about your own bullet still lodged in your flesh?

First things first.

Seven days pass before I visit the *comedor* again and can check on leg-wound man. All week I stew about his festering lesion. I dream about his screams. I light candles in my house. Every time I pass a candle, I think about leg-wound man. The next week I find out that this fellow is doing better. Much better.

I am stunned. The miracle of drugs. And youth.

We pitch in and buy them both a bus ticket home. One fellow still has a bullet in his rear end but seems OK. He'll have it taken care of eventually.

Remind me to stay off of trains in Sinaloa. And remind me to stick close to Ricardo, who knows how to come up with strategies when I am immobilized. And remind me to learn from the expertise, loving care and ingenuity of Nurse Norma, who could function with calm effectiveness anywhere on the planet.

LESSONS FROM FRANCISCO

Padre Francisco has six weeks left at *el comedor*. He arrived almost one year ago, and as part of his novice experience as a Jesuit he has worked closely with the issues of immigration. I was fairly new as a Samaritan volunteer when Francisco arrived. In fact, I thought for several weeks that Francisco was a migrant himself. Mopping the floors and carrying in huge sacks of potatoes, he didn't look like a priest. With his ponytail and beard, his jeans and his hoodie, and his housekeeping duties, I was surprised to learn that this period at the *comedor* was a portion of his training to become a Jesuit priest.

Today we chat for a few minutes before all the duties of managing the growing group of migrants envelop us both. It is a pleasant, cool morning and we lean against a car in front of el *comedor*.

—*mm*—

Francisco is reflective.

"This place has changed us, no?"

I agree. Sometimes the helpers learn more than the helpees.

"So, how has this place changed you?" I ask Francisco.

He smiles and his answer sticks with me. "I used to believe that God created the universe. Now I think that God and man are creating the universe together."

So all of what evolves on the planet is an ongoing sort of process? God and man working together? Nice. Not the old *deus ex machina* theory where God steps in and saves the day. Instead, for Francisco the idea is that what we do has a lot of impact on how the world turns. Sometimes it feels like so little—peeling potatoes for the evening meal or coming up with a few dollars for a bus ticket home for a migrant. These small acts of kindness feel pretty insignificant when placed against the hundreds of people I see weekly who have lost everything.

But seeing the way the travelers trudge out the door of the *comedor* with a clean pair of socks in one hand and hearing their words of gratitude as they pass by, well, I am the one who receives the most profound gift. It is the gift of seeing their dignity and courage, the gift of watching them put their own life on the line for their children and family. They are my heroes.

We murmur to each other "*Vaya con Dios*" and "*Buena suerte.* (good luck).

For a brief moment in time, the world is a better place.

I ask Francisco why he wanted to become a priest.

"The most important thing for me is education and service to the poor," he tells me, looking at the long line of pilgrims gathering before breakfast at the door of shelter.

"And, yes, the Mass and the spirit are necessary, too, but the main driving force for me is education and helping those in need in my country."

I suggest that he is giving up a lot by entering the priesthood. He smiles and talks about the trade-offs in all of life's choices. He will miss having a family and children. But he looks at the morning crowd of migrants waiting for breakfast and says, "I guess these are my children."

There are difficulties no matter how we choose to live a life. Living with the Jesuit brothers is something Francisco enjoys, but he tells me that the Jesuit life has many complications and conflicts as well. He is lucky that he can make a choice about how to live his life. So many of the migrants do not have this option.

A couple of today's weary travelers vie for his attention, so Francisco shuffles his papers and pencils and begins to process the lineup of exhausted, hungry migrants. So many papers, so much documentation necessary for the undocumented. The paperwork would drive me crazy, but he puts his shoulder to the wheel and offers his hand and a smile.

"¿*Qué tal, amigo?*" (How's it going, friend?)

In Francisco's worldview, the main problems of Mexico are indifference, corruption, fear, greed and poverty. He talks about the gap between the rich and the poor, and the fact that the rich don't care.

"I try to put a little seed into the ground and plant it." He stomps his foot on the ground to make sure I understand. He repeats: "Plant a seed." "If we can do this each day," he says, "the world will be a better place, no?"

We decide to keep in touch. Francisco will be off to Cuernavaca soon. It will be my pleasure to follow his career as a Jesuit priest. He is a person who makes a difference no matter where he is placed. He will bloom where he is planted.

SOME FRESH AIR

Showing up each week at the *comedor* and pitching in with the various tasks at hand has been both exhilarating and frustrating. I often ask myself what this small output of energy is really doing in terms of the big picture. How is this activity affecting the complicated and ineffectual U.S. immigration policies that are operating on the border? Is this the best use of my time?

The answers to many such questions lie in the idealism of college students who are passionate about the border and immigration issues. For two years the Santa Cruz Community Foundation was the sponsoring agency for a summer immersion program. Then the Border Community Alliance (BCA) took over this unique program. BCA is a nonprofit organization dedicated to supporting social, cultural and economic development in the borderlands. It is a genuine bicultural effort governed by Mexican and United States stakeholders. As a BCA board member, I had the pleasure and challenge of coordinating the intern program.

The enthusiasm, energy and intelligence of the interns were the perfect antidote to my frustrations regarding America's direction of increased militarization and border security. These young people plunged into border politics with open hearts and impressive courage. In just a few short weeks they were involved in some powerful activities. Most of the border interns were fluent in Spanish and so were able to have in-depth conversations with the migrant population.

One thing that has become very clear to me as I work with the migrants is that I do not understand how to affect the political processes that dictate social change. Even though inhumane treatment and social injustice scream out to me each week when I talk with deported migrants, I have difficulty seeing how I can change policy in any major way. It is the young people, the students who are passionate about Latin America and immigration rights, who will push for the changes we so desperately need in our immigration system. They will figure out just and humane answers.

Together the interns and I traveled to the *comedor* each week, went on desert searches and drove to conferences and local demonstrations on the immigration crisis in Arizona. One student wrote his graduate thesis while plunging into the murky politics of the border. Another created a documentary film about the migrant experience. Bringing some light and hope to my efforts at the *comedor*, they all became totally devoted to bringing about change in the borderlands. The experience was life-changing for them. It gave me optimism about the future.

One event we attended was a picnic for a group of American border advocates doing the Migrant Trail Walk, an annual event that brings attention to the number of deaths in the desert. The Samaritans provided a picnic lunch for the sixty Migrant Trail participants who were hiking a known migrant trail from Sasabe, Arizona, to Tucson, in some ways replicating the journey of so many pilgrims traveling north. I brought Ryan, a graduate student at the University of San Francisco, to the event. It was a very hot June day as we drove to a remote encampment deep in the desert.

―――

On our way to the encampment, we encounter a migrant from Honduras who walks into a gas station where our Samaritan group is fueling up our vehicles. He asks for a ride to Tucson. Clearly he is in trouble. He has been

Peg Bowden with border interns Nina Foushee and Ryan Murphy in El Paso, Texas, 2012

walking for seven days, most of the time alone. During the past two days he has seen two dead bodies in the desert. In the past twenty-four hours he has been followed by a pack of coyotes—the four-legged variety. He is dehydrated, limping from blisters on his feet and traumatized. He looks to be about twenty years old. The young Honduran traveler joins our group and we take him with us to the picnic lunch, where he is immediately hydrated and fed.

The young man is sitting in a folding chair in the shade of a mesquite tree examining his bleeding feet. It's a hundred degrees in the shade, and there is no wind. He smiles wanly as I approach him at the picnic site.

My intern Ryan has spent the past two years in Honduras working in an orphanage, so he bonds immediately with our young guest. Ryan gives him his backpack, and one of the Migrant Trail Walkers gives him a pair of shoes. I give him fresh socks and treat his feet as best I can with the supplies I have in my backpack. One of the Samaritans gives our migrant friend a T-shirt with our Samaritan logo printed on the front.

It is a riveting experience for Ryan. Our Honduran friend is trying to walk to Phoenix because his girlfriend has just given birth to their first baby, a son. He just wants to see his son. He was deported eight months before. When I ask what he will do after meeting his new son, he says he isn't sure.

"Maybe return to Honduras. I have a job there and can send money to Phoenix."

There is fire and determination in this young man. He is willing to die or be imprisoned just for a glimpse of his son.

THE YOUNG AND THE BRAVE

One cloudless day in late June, I went on a desert search with seasoned Samaritan Mike Casey and Nina, an intern from Stanford University. After waking at 4:30 a.m. and meeting the desert search team, we arrived at our rendezvous point at dawn. For excursions into the desert, early mornings offer a welcome alternative to the the scorching temperatures of the afternoon.

We sipped our coffee in the van and smelled the pungent creosote bush that permeated the morning air after last night's rain. Vermilion flycatchers and pyrrhuloxias, the desert cardinals, were darting through the mesquite trees as we scanned the horizon for migrants who might need our help.

The desert was coming to life after a few good rains during the past week. Ocotillos, a spiny Arizona cactus with occasional leaves and bright red flowers, were leafing out. *Mal mujer*, or "wicked wife," an alluring white flower surrounded by deep green foliage that stings to the touch and appears only during the hottest days of summer, was flourishing on the side of the road.

Mike, our search guide, decided to take us to an encampment run by No More Deaths (NMD), a nonprofit organization that has been an important presence in the desert. This activist group also does searches, water drops and advocacy for immigration reform. Members of NMD are mostly in their twenties, many of them college students seeking an experience that acquaints them with the immigration issues of the borderlands. They operate a campsite that assists injured and exhausted migrants. Getting to this campsite was an adventure in itself: A rutted gravel road with steep grades slowed our van to a crawl. We bounced and lurched in the van, dodging deep ruts and muddied *arroyos* left over from the recent monsoon rains. Mike was masterful at maneuvering the van around ditches and crevices.

The altar of migrant treasures, No More Deaths Camp.

The campsite is set on acreage owned by Byrd Baylor, a famous author of children's books and lifelong resident of Arizona. My own children were raised on Byrd Baylor's books, which are wonderful tales of native spirit and desert lore. Byrd has been caring for these travelers of the desert for decades and is fierce about protecting them, often in defiance of law enforcement.

~~~

We pull into the NMD camp during late morning and are greeted by several young women who offer to give us a tour of their operation. The camp consists of several large tents—a medical tent, the kitchen tent, a pantry, a tent that stores clothing and shoes, and a pit toilet over yonder. Several small sleeping tents surround the encampment. Solar panels and batteries supply energy for a swamp cooler in the medical tent and for lights at night. One young man, a medical student from the University of Rochester in New York, is here for several months. He is treating four migrant men who staggered in a few hours before our arrival. The migrants are dehydrated and suffering from hyperthermia, or elevated body temperature. Sitting under a shaded *ramada* and glancing at us furtively, they look dusty, exhausted and frightened.

We do our best not to disturb the medical interventions that are taking place during our visit. The migrant patients are clearly nervous and suspicious about our presence in the camp.

I am impressed with the organization of this aid station and the commitment shown by these young people in offering this service. This is summer, and they could be on a beach somewhere relaxing with a cold brew. The heat is oppressive on this day, and the volunteers are flushed and look drained.

There is no relief from the heat at this outpost. The shade is scarce, and the tents are stifling. I think about the TV series *M*A*S*H* and the medical improvisation that evolves in harsh conditions. Today there is a helicopter circling overhead, and the volunteers are edgy as they figure the Border Patrol has spotted the migrants huddled in the medical tent. When a Border Patrol agent whizzes by on the road in an all-terrain vehicle at one point, the tension at the camp rises exponentially.

The medical student from New York has worked at this camp before. Dressed in a stained silky bicycle shirt, he looks as if he has been lost in the desert himself. He was the medical presence at this campsite the previous summer and also came for a few weeks at Christmas. I ask him why he is drawn to this experience.

"I'm probably learning more here than any medical school can offer," comes his thoughtful reply after he reflects on this for a moment. We are standing in the sun at high noon. I can barely tolerate the high temperatures, but our doctor friend seems perfectly comfortable.

We discuss the protocols for blistered feet, dehydration and gastric upsets. Many migrants drink tainted water from stock tanks for cattle during their journey and arrive with severe diarrhea and gastroenteritis. We compare notes about emergency treatment for dehydration and common injuries sustained while hiking in the desert.

Leaving the NMD camp, I notice a sign at the entrance that reads, "No More Deaths, *Bienvenidos*" (welcome). The sign is painted on an old blue car door, and two gallon jugs of water lie beside the sign. A short distance away there is a blue flag waving, visible for miles. A lost desert traveler can spot this beacon of hope and receive life-giving support.

The NMD camp is definitely a place for the young and the strong. We never discussed politics with the volunteers. The politics of saving lives is reduced to profound simplicity. When a person is dying in the desert, you do everything you can to save a life.

BROTHERLY LOVE

The first-aid station in Nogales is no longer across the street from the *comedor*. Now it is about a half-mile up the road. Services and activities change rapidly on the border, depending on the numbers of deportees, the presence of criminals preying on the vulnerable migrants, and the politics of the day. The Samaritans have learned to be flexible when an agency closes and another one opens. Now the first-aid needs of the migrants have been displaced to another location. We all scramble and try to figure out how best to help.

Walking along a busy city street with trucks and taxis whizzing by, it is not an easy stroll from the *comedor* to the new first-aid station. This is especially true in the heat of the summer, when the street asphalt reflects the soaring temperatures. Small *taquerías* and fruit stands with tarps strung up for shade offer some Mexican hospitality for the strollers. Since one cannot take fruit and produce across the border back into the United States, we are not usually customers at these venues.

—⁓—

One day a small group of pale, overheated Samaritans slowly make their way back to the *comedor* after working at the first-aid station. It is noon and the sun is intense and relentless, with no shade on the street. The proprietor of the fruit stand approaches our little red-faced group with a platter of freshly cut watermelon and insists we each take a slice. He comments on the heat and wants us to sit in the shade for a moment and enjoy his offering. It is a lovely moment for me, as I have wanted to buy something from his small stand for months. And now he is giving us a sample.

He would accept no money for this offering. Clearly

enjoying the way we all dive into the watermelon, he just smiles and thanks us for "the work." He sees my Samaritan T-shirt, and like many Mexicans I meet, he expresses his gratitude for our efforts. We walk away with sticky fingers and many exchanges of "*Gracias*" and "*De nada.*" Frequently I experience many pleasant spontaneous moments of generosity and hospitality in Mexico, and I always walk away with a smile.

Crossing back into *Los Estados Unidos* is usually a different story. "Step back," a Border Patrol agent commands if I've ventured too close to the person ahead of me who is being processed at the port of entry.

"What is in your backpack?" asks the Customs agent in a polite official tone. "What have you bought? Where have you gone in Mexico? Please remove your sunglasses." As the agent busies himself with my passport and his computer, federal marshals walk about with their weapons slung over their shoulders.

I try to direct my mind elsewhere. I think about watermelon and Mexican salsa music as I wait in the hot sun. I try to make friendly conversation.

"The watermelon at that stand over there is incredible. You ought to give it a try sometime," I casually offer.

"I've never been over there," the Customs agent replies.

"You ought to give it a try sometime."

He just looks at me and shrugs.

LIVIN' THE DREAM

In the San Cayetano Mountains, our home is perched on

the edge of a canyon with a small river at its base that attracts birds. It is the perfect stopover for birds on the wing heading back and forth from Mexico to the United States. We have become birdwatchers, and my husband goes through huge sacks of birdseed each month at our feeders. I hear the gentle swoosh of the birdseed at 5 a.m. as he fills the feeders on his morning rounds.

Generally, during eleven months of the year the species are strictly segregated at the feeders. The finches are the first to arrive in the morning, and the cowbirds and doves crowd them out as the day wears on. The orioles drain the hummingbird feeders of nectar. A family of shy cardinals creeps in as the sun goes down after the rest of the flocks have gone to their nesting places. Indeed, the birds of a feather really do flock together.

But when June arrives and the desert is parched, something strange and wonderful happens. All the species share the feeders side by side. There is no acrimony when the temperatures soar and the pickin's are slim. I see cardinals next to buntings and grosbeaks next to tanagers. Everyone gets along. There is communal bathing at the birdbath, with the aggressive cowbirds taking a dip with the lesser goldfinch.

When the chips are down, it is a virtual United Nations of birds.

But then come the rains of summer, and flowers, grasses and seeds flourish within weeks. The desert floor that looked baked and cracked quickly turns green and lush and becomes tangled in vines and blossoms. Insects appear and the flycatchers get fat and happy. The hummingbirds are in a frenzy, dive-bombing each other in their war games as

Illegal immigrants of the Bible.

they skim the fields of flowers. The birds are back to their clannish ways. They stick to their own kind.

In these early hot weeks of the summer of 2012, just when the desert floor was scorched and the numbers of migrant deaths were rising, there was a human breakthrough—a moment of relief. There was some peace and dialogue at the metaphorical birdbath. President Obama issued an executive order proclaiming that people who arrived in the United States as children, attended our schools, and perhaps served in our military, were not to be deported. These are the "DREAM kids," and there is a guarded optimism about Obama's proclamation. DREAM is an acronym for Development, Relief and Education for Alien Minors.

THE DREAMERS

Not long after the president's directive, I volunteered at a high school in Tucson to assist young DREAMers with the paperwork and documentation necessary to apply for deferred action and the possibility of employment. One thousand people showed up the first night of this registration process.

It was early September and the high school cafeteria was sweltering, loud and chaotic, but there was order and respect in the room as well. Families were patient; some waited in line four hours. No one complained. This directive has given hope to tens of thousands of people who have lived under the radar, afraid to expose their birthplaces.

The media were present, with TV cameras and reporters crowding into the school cafeteria. Margo Cowan, a Tucson attorney and organizer of this effort, politely asked them to leave. Many parents were anxious about their safety. They and their children were undocumented and only wanted to assure a secure future in this country for their families. The TV cameras and reporters left the cafeteria, and we all plunged into the tedious business of filling out the long, complicated forms.

I assisted a family of three young men accompanied by their father. They entered the United States from Ciudad Juarez, Mexico, in 2001 with visitors' visas but failed to renew them. This family did not want to return to Ciudad Juarez for the visa renewal process.

The father explained to me, "I could not keep my boys in Juarez. It is a dangerous place."

Carrying three file folders with pages of school transcripts, birth certificates and addresses of residences, the father, his three sons and I waded through the lengthy, confusing application forms titled "Consideration of Deferred Action for Childhood Arrivals." At times it was like slogging through mud.

"And where did you move after August 2003 and before 2006," I asked. "And then where did you live after 2006? ... What about those four months in spring 2007? ... Have you ever been arrested for a crime in this country? ... Do you belong to a gang?"

When I mentioned gangs, the boys' father shouted, "No!" He pounded his fist on the table.

"My boys are good boys! They will make something of themselves," their father's voice boomed across the noisy cafeteria.

Each place of residence was carefully listed. The father did his best to remember the addresses of the apartments and trailer parks where they lived before moving into the house they now rent. There were small piles of bills and credit-card records proving he and the boys lived in this

PHOTO: MARTY ETHINGTON

DREAMers on the march in Nogales, Mexico, July 2013

country. He beamed as he showed me the photos of his boys on their old visas when they were younger.

Dad was tearful when we shook hands and parted after an hour of detailed interrogation and filling out of forms. I thanked him for gathering all the documentation so carefully. It had taken him three weeks and a dozen trips to the library copy machine to complete the folders. I shook the boys' hands, and their father gave me a hug. They were so happy.

For a moment, I think, we all felt a little bit closer to the American dream. But we were also cautiously optimistic. Let us not forget that President Obama has deported more undocumented migrants than any other president in history.

~~~

On one of my weekly trips to the *comedor* after the president's proclamation, I look for potential DREAMers, young people who have been deported yet think of the United States as their homeland, their roots. There are no DREAMer candidates on this day, but there are two children, ages nine and eleven, who tell the Samaritans they are heading to New York City to find their father. They are accompanied by their aunt, a woman who is nineteen years old.

I am horrified. It is one of the hottest days of the summer, and these youngsters are determined to cross the border wall and find their father, who is more than two thousand miles away. One of the Samaritans gives the nine-year-old boy a sheet of paper and crayons and asks him to draw his journey thus far. The drawing is poignant. He draws himself and a wall, and up in the corner he draws a tiny figure—his father—surrounded by tall buildings.

We show the aunt and the two youngsters a map depicting the distance to New York City and talk about the number of days it takes to walk from Nogales to Tucson. We speak of the number of bottles of water each person must drink every day. We show them a map with red dots depicting the number of deaths that have occurred in the desert. The children listen politely. They do not respond to our concerns. They are young and invulnerable and are on a great adventure to find their father. The little boy tells us it has been a long time since he has seen his father.

"I just want to know him," he says as he draws his papa. I am lost in this child's eyes.

It is hell hot, with the clicking ceiling fans barely

making a dent in the heavy sultriness on this summer morning. We are all milling around, migrants and Samaritans, the Jesuit priests and the Sisters of the Eucharist, in a kind of stupor of heat and confusion. As the children and their aunt leave the *comedor,* we alert one of the sisters about this tragedy in the making. The trio is sleeping tonight at *Casa Nazaret.*

As I watch this drama unfold, it occurs to me that there is no way we can know how many migrants are crossing the desert, much less how many never make it. There have been six thousand bodies recovered since 1994. The desert is a vast graveyard for the nameless and the lost.

Several days after my encounter with the children and their aunt, I hear that they have crossed and are walking in the desert near Sasabe, Arizona, a tiny border outpost. The temperature that day is 103. I say a silent prayer for these young children and try to visualize a future for them.

JOSÉ

Summer's end was near, and back-to-school thoughts were on the minds of children and parents. In the U.S. young men were seen on school athletic fields preparing for the fall football season. School marching bands were practicing in the early evening hours, when it was cooler.

I meet José at the *comedor* sitting on one of the long benches. Tears are flowing and he is trying to be as inconspicuous as possible. José is fourteen and was recently picked up in the desert with his mother while crossing the border in an attempt to return to their home in Chicago. He is a handsome boy and wears a rosary around his neck. José has lived in Chicago since he was twelve months old, brought to the Windy City by his parents as a baby. Proudly telling me he attends a prestigious academy in Chicago, José begins to cry again. He is on the student council and is chairman of the committee that plans the eighth-grade graduation. José is heartbroken because he cannot return to his home and his life, and he doesn't understand why.

This young man and his mother traveled to Jalisco, Mexico, where his grandmother was dying. It was his first trip to Mexico since he was an infant. Because José had never met his grandmother, his mother wanted him to see the matriarch of the family before she died. And he did. Grandmother died a few weeks ago, and now José and his mother are trying to get back to Chicago.

If ever there was a poster child for the DREAM Act, this child is the perfect candidate. He speaks very little Spanish; his primary language is English. He does not identify with Mexico as his home or birthplace. José loves Chicago, is a White Sox fan and lives a short distance from my own girlhood home on the South Side. My emotions were unbalanced while talking with this young man, and I had to walk away to stop my tears.

The tragedy is this: Because José and his mother have been gone during the summer months, tending to their grandmother in her final days, they are not eligible to apply for the deferred action status that allows young people who grew up in the United States to stay in this country without fear of deportation. He cannot apply as a DREAM kid because they have tried to enter the United States without proper documentation. They have been gone from their home in Chicago for too many months.

José has an aunt in Tijuana, Mexico, and so the Samaritans quickly empty their wallets and buy them both bus tickets. Using a borrowed cell phone, he calls his aunt in Tijuana, and I hear him tell her about "these nice people helping us." Later that night José calls one of the Samaritans to tell us he is safe and on his way to Tijuana.

The enormity of pain and human tragedy is difficult to quantify. A young man is in tears. He is an honor student at a superior academy in Chicago. He and his mother almost lost their lives in the desert. He has lived in the United States since he was a baby. This experience will affect this young man in ways no one can predict.

When I returned home from the *comedor* that day, I wrote President Obama and my congressional representative. Then I wrote the principal of José's school in Chicago. I try to visualize José in ten years and imagine him graduating from college and even running for a political office. I hope it is here in the United States. He is a leader. Good things will come to him.

A few weeks later, the Samaritans call José from the *comedor*; luckily we kept his cell-phone number. He is in Tijuana with his aunt and his mother. We ask him to write his story— the story of his journey from Chicago to the Arizona desert to detention to the *comedor* to Tijuana. He promises that he will do this and send it to us. José sounds hopeful and still talks about returning to his school in Chicago.

Days later I receive a letter from my congressional representative expressing his sadness at his inability to offer concrete help to José. He gives me a list of Arizona attorneys who may offer guidance in this situation.

I think about this child every day.

LOVE STORIES

In midsummer I spent several hours at an airport, heading to a city more than a thousand miles from my Arizona home. For a short time I was a pilgrim, traveling along with thousands of others to different parts of the United States. I was on the move, migrating.

Airports are a microcosm of the human condition. I see children racing up and down the concourse, parents arguing, lovers embracing and a woman sobbing uncontrollably as she speaks into her cell phone. So many stories, so many dramas.

Traveling to see my daughter and grandchild, I smile in expectation. I put up with the hassles of air travel such as the shoes-off, shoes-on maneuvering in the security line. Grumbling when I pay $11 for a soggy chicken sandwich, I silently curse the airport for scalping travelers. I question all these Homeland Security regulations as I take off my shoes, my belt, my jacket and my silver bracelet and drop my carry-on bag several times. But as always, eventually I get through the dance of airport security and dream of landing in a far-off place.

Traveling to see family is an accepted ritual for most

Americans. We hop on a plane or gas up the car and off we go, usually several times a year if our family lives at a distance. We Skype, we e-mail, we talk on the telephone. We are a restless bunch.

Rarely do we stay in one town or one home for more than ten years. We move to chase after economic security and a better job. We move to be close to our children and grandchildren. We move to get away from people we hate; we move to be close to people we love. Or we move because we love new places, new people, new challenges. And we move because we can. It's a free country. We can live where we choose.

In contrast, my migrant friends at the *comedor* move because they are desperately seeking economic survival. Some are being threatened by cartels and gangs. They are torn between staying in their villages and moving to *Los Estados Unidos*, a land of plenty. Some young men from Honduras told me that this is what you do when you are a teenager. You come to America. Life will be better.

Another reason you migrate to America is for love. Every migrant I meet at *el comedor* has someone he or she loves in Mexico, the United States or, most often, both places. The *comedor* is a place filled with passionate, tragic love stories of people seeking their children, their spouses, their lovers. Families become separated. People are torn.

—◆—

One chilly morning I meet Eric, a roofing contractor from California. He is standing in front of the *comedor* in a T-shirt. It is forty degrees. Eric has been in a U.S. detention

We're family.

center for weeks and was deported to Nogales at four this morning. His jacket was confiscated during his detention time and he is hoping the Samaritans have some warm jackets this morning.

And we do. Shoes, too. I watch him try on an almost-new pair of Adidas shoes and look over the pile of men's clothing. He is a big man, bigger than most of the other men. He finds a well-insulated jacket and squeezes into it. The sleeves are too short and the zipper doesn't work, but he takes the jacket and looks for some clean socks.

"Where is your home?" I ask him as he sorts through a pile of jeans.

Instead of answering, he asks, "Can I show you pictures of my family?"

He pulls a worn plastic bag out of his beat-up duffel bag and carefully removes Christmas cards with photographs tucked inside. There is a reverence as he carefully spreads the photos on the breakfast table. I can feel his yearning to be with the people in these photos.

Eric introduces me to his family: three sons. The youngest is graduating from high school in California and is decked out in his school uniform. The middle son has on an ROTC uniform full of medals and stripes, and Eric tells me this boy is a sophomore in college. The third son is dressed in camouflage fatigues and is stationed at Fort Benning.

I ask Eric, "Why are you here?"

"I was driving without a license." He shrugs. The sort of shrug indicating that he messed up big-time, and he knows it.

"So what is your plan?"

"I have to get to California. I must see my son graduate from high school." His eyes cloud up as he tells me this.

I take out my camera and take his photo by a mural of the *Virgen de Guadalupe,* a popular photo-op spot, and I tell Eric to be careful. The desert is dangerous, and he is vulnerable if he travels alone. He is still staring at the photos of his sons and fingers the images as we speak. He is not listening to me.

Eric tells me that his parents and family live in Guerrero but that he has lived in *Los Estados Unidos* for nineteen years and has steady work as a roofer. He gives me a hug, thanks me for the clothes, crosses himself and heads out the door.

─◠◠◠◠─

I think about the numbers of people I have met at *el comedor* who have children in one country and a spouse, a family or a sweetheart in another. Risking their lives to cross the desert, they live under the radar to be with family and work in the United States. And yet, also having parents, a spouse or children back in Mexico, my migrant friends are torn and conflicted. Often they are desperate to see loved ones.

Many have not seen their wives, husbands or children for years. They are truly stuck in the complexities and legal labyrinth of a broken immigration system. They have been living in the United States, often sending money back to Mexico or quietly supporting their families in California, Nebraska, or maybe Texas. Now they are stuck in Nogales. Many will attempt to cross and cross and cross again and again to reach their loved ones. The separation tears them apart emotionally.

There is no wall that will stop them.

Trust me on this.

I remember the film *Sophie's Choice*, with Meryl Streep. Set in Nazi Poland during World War II, the film tells of the unimaginable choice Sophie has to make, giving up one of her children to a Nazi SS officer in order to save the other. It is a film that still haunts me.

I see that same haunted look in the eyes of the men and women today. They are forced to make choices that most of us will never have to make. They are driven by love. Logic has nothing to do with it. It is a drive beyond reason. I often watch my Samaritan colleagues doing their best to talk the migrants out of crossing the desert.

"Go back to your villages. We will help with bus money and food. The journey is too long and difficult."

And I know that these brave and lost souls will follow their hearts and walk as many miles as it takes, sleep in as many thorny *arroyos* as they must, to reach California or Tennessee or New York.

So they patiently go through the piles of clothes, pick out some clean socks and gratefully accept packets of toiletries to make their lives a bit more bearable.

I watch the children and teenagers at the *comedor* today. Kids are much more in the moment than adults. Their presence always lightens the mood somehow. Little Rosalia shows me her pink backpack and feeds the resident kitty.

Adriana, age thirteen, introduces me to her big brother and her mother. They are from Veracruz and have been walking in the desert for seven days. I ask where they are heading.

"Houston. Then we'll go to New York," Adriana replies. "We must see our papa again."

The Samaritans borrow a cell phone and call Adriana's papa in New York. I watch her jumping up and down as she tells her father that she will see him soon. Once again I shake my head in disbelief and fear for this little family.

I learn about the power of love each time I visit the *comedor*. Love can make us crazy and irrational and obsessed, and these travelers teach me powerful lessons about all of this once again. I see the love that emanates from the Jesuit priests and the Sisters of the Eucharist who serve the migrants. I see the love shining in the eyes of the migrants as they tell me about their families and sweethearts whom they miss and dream of.

Love is alive and well and permeates every inch of *el comedor*. It is a force more powerful than any wall or fence that divides us.

THE DOUBLE-EDGED SWORD

The North American Free Trade Agreement (NAFTA), which is a treaty among Canada, the United States and Mexico, has been an economic success for the United States. It has been a financial disaster, however, for the small farms of central and southern Mexico. NAFTA has allowed U.S. government-subsidized products and produce to flood Mexico, creating negative consequences throughout Latin America. Small farmers cannot compete with the artificially low prices of corn, rice and other produce grown on the huge farms in the United States, Mexico and countries farther south.

In the seven years after NAFTA was implemented, 1994

to 2001, Mexico's poverty level nearly doubled, from 16 percent to 28 percent of the total national population. The sale of corn, a staple crop of Mexico for millennia, was disrupted because of the imports of U.S. corn, which were sold at a much lower price through farm subsidies. This had a significant bearing on the livelihood of the Mexican farming community.[9]

I estimate that half or more of the migrants I meet each week at the *comedor* are migrating for economic reasons. They are farmers and have cultivated their land for generations. Their village cultures and family lives have revolved around the planting, cultivating and harvesting of crops native to their regions, especially corn. Farming without the use of pesticides on small parcels of land, they have learned how to survive and sustain their rural livelihood year after year. They cannot compete with the large U.S. agribusinesses that have developed in and near their villages since the enactment of NAFTA.

"I cannot return to my farm now, because of the chemicals and poisons that have destroyed the soil," they tell me.

U.S. agribusinesses have poured their pesticides and chemicals into the rich farmland, which is rapidly becoming depleted.[10] As Mexicans lost their farms, they moved north, often working for low wages and poor conditions in the *maquiladora* program. *Maquiladoras* are foreign-owned factories in Mexico. The migrants I meet are not factory workers; they are farmers. They struggle to figure out the next step in their survival.

I first notice a couple of pilgrims at the *comedor* sweeping floors, serving food and scrubbing out the toilets. They are migrants from Puebla, Mexico, and they immediately throw themselves into the day-to-day chores of the shelter. Mariana and Armando are a couple and come from a family of farmers who have been cultivating tomatoes, corn, beans and chilies for generations. They sell the produce to villages surrounding their home, and their lives have revolved around the seasons. Planting, harvesting, going to market and producing high-quality grains and vegetables has been a good living for their families. It is what they know.

Both were forced to migrate to *el norte* because they could no longer support their family. They have left their three young children back in Puebla with grandparents. I notice that Mariana never smiles. Armando never sits down. They are hard workers, and soon KBI offers them jobs. Armando will be the night watchman; Mariana will help with the food preparation and service and the cleanup tasks at the *comedor*.

Mariana and Armando's story is a direct result of NAFTA. Huge corporate NAFTA-sanctioned agribusinesses engulfed their farming activities in Puebla. After years of trying, they could not compete.

―――

Monsanto, DuPont and Dow, all agribusiness giants, have planted millions of acres of genetically modified corn in Latin America. They are lobbying to plant this genetically altered maize in Sinaloa and Chiapas. Food raised using genetically modified engineering methods is a controversial topic, a double-edged sword. Those favoring organic, unmodified methods warn of the lack of research regarding the long-range implications of altering food at the genetic level. Flooding the market with genetically modified foods may destroy the fragile balance of insects and microorganisms that is helpful in food production. Some studies involving rats linked cancerous tumors and infertility to the ingesting of genetically modified organisms. Severe allergies have been found in people who consume GMO corn and other altered foods.

Those who favor GMO foods point to the fact that the plants are resistant to pests and the crops are more plentiful. It is the answer to world hunger. The huge bounties of corn and other staples will feed millions of people.

At issue is the fact that in Mexico, GMO corn cross-pollinates with non-GMO corn in nearby fields, thus destroying the diverse, native maize that has been the staple food of millions in Latin America for hundreds of years. Native plants and even weeds are contaminated with GMO-tainted pollen. Superweeds develop, resistant to herbicides, and choke out needed crops. We have disrupted methods of subsistence farming that have sustained generations of people in favor of a model that lines the pockets of Monsanto and DuPont.[11]

—*mm*—

Mariana and Armando tried to cross the border to find work in the U.S. They were picked up by the Border Patrol. Separated and taken to different detention centers, Mariana was released after one day, but Armando remained in the prison facility for seven days. Mariana could not find him and sought refuge at *el comedor*. Both are now in Nogales trying to decide on their next step. For over a year Mariana has lived in the women's shelter, *Casa Nazaret*. Armando sleeps in the shelter at night as he performs his duties as night watchman. It has been fifteen months since this couple has seen their three small children.

Mariana speaks very little English. Each week she and I peel potatoes or sort through the clothes. I teach her some English, and she tells me the Spanish words for "backpack" and "socks."

Our Samaritan group has adopted this hard-working couple and I am humbled by the sacrifices they have made for their children. Sometimes I see Mariana off in a corner quietly crying. She sells paper cones of gelatin to passing tourists at the port of entry when she is not serving the migrants at the *comedor*. She agonizes about being in Nogales when her children are 1,000 miles away.

The Samaritans give Armando a decent sleeping bag and a CD player for his long nights as watchman. After watching this drama unfold over a year, we all chip in and buy Mariana a round-trip bus ticket to Puebla. She is a picture of maternal ecstasy when she returns after several weeks at home with her children. This is not an easy road for the family, but their tenacity and hard work give me pause to think about what is truly important in life.

Watching the lives of Mariana and Armando makes me think about my own good fortune. I have never known a day when I couldn't feed myself or my children. True, there were times when we ate a lot of beans or macaroni and cheese. But why was I born into a home of middle-class affluence and not in a *barrio* a few miles across the Mexican border where I would have known only poverty and suffering? Are people poor because they don't work hard? Do they somehow deserve their plight?

I believe extraneous circumstances create poverty. Economic and immigration policies, lack of education, even lack of birth control—all these dynamics create situations involving suffering and financial hardship. A healthy economy is a benevolent economy. The consumer prospers and so does the businessman. Sound economic policies allow both sides to prosper. It is no more complex than that.

A market economy must have a moral thread. It looks at consequences. It provides products at reasonable prices for reasonable profits; it pays workers fairly and treats them well; it serves the communities to which it belongs. It is a win-win.

A fair market acts responsibly toward itself, the family, the community, the country and the world.

I confess I am an insufferable idealist.

The NAFTA design needs better protections. We have lower gas prices and cheaper tomatoes thanks to NAFTA. Because of NAFTA, we import a lot of our oil from Mexico. Shipping produce north to the United States is therefore cheaper because gasoline costs are contained.[12]

However, the huge waves of migrant crossings into the United States are a direct result of NAFTA. Large numbers of indigenous farmers from Oaxaca, Chiapas, Jalisco and Central America arrive at the *comedor* each week. We have created a new class of poverty in Mexico, a group that had survived for many generations until faced with free trade agreements.

At the same time, trade agreements are a necessity for the United States when competing in a more globalized world. We need to rethink NAFTA and consider the humanitarian impact of our policies. Instead of *free* trade, we need *fair* trade.

I watch Mariana as she spends days washing dishes, sweeping floors and selling gelatin to tourists in fancy recreational vehicles. The quiet dignity that Armando and Mariana display is a testament to the power of love and faith—love of family and faith that tomorrow will be better.

My migrant friends teach me patience each day. The Spanish word *esperar* means two things: "to wait" and "to hope." I see the dynamic of *esperanza*, or hope, in the eyes of every migrant. Their chance is coming. They know it. They will wait until the time is right, and then they will take that chance.

In July the Samaritans help Armando travel to Puebla and bring his children to Nogales. The reunited family now has a small apartment, and little Brian, age three, spends time at the *comedor* on Tuesdays with the Samaritans. We are teaching him English. The older children are in school, and Armando tells me they are *muy contento* (very content). This is one love story with a happy ending.

Mariana and Armando teach me that there is more to life than material wealth, the clutter of our lives. The bonds of family and friends are profound. I hear stories of migrants risking their lives for each other. Many give up their chance for freedom in order to help a friend in the desert. The adversity and tragedy of my migrant friends' lives invoke the best and sometimes the worst in what human behavior is all about.

A SONG IN MY HEART

Toward the end of summer, there was a last spurt of monsoon activity. Rain poured each day, and the grasses of late summer began to flourish again on the desert floor. During one of these sporadic storms, the Samaritans were sorting clothing at the *comedor* while the migrants queued up outside, waiting patiently. They were getting wet in this surprise summer deluge and so came back into the shelter to stay dry. We were crowded in the tiny space, and the men closely lined up at the side of the room in four rows.

—*mm*—

I comment that the men look like a choir, albeit a bedraggled and wet choir. The rain is beating down on the tin roof, and suddenly the room is filled with song.

The men begin to sing with gusto, huge smiles on their faces. The song is "*Cielito Lindo* (Heavenly Sweet One),"[13] a popular Mexican love song. It is one of those spontaneous, unscripted moments that touch everyone's heart. When the men reach the chorus of "*Ay, ay, ay, ay, canta y no llores* (Sing and don't cry)," most people in the room join in. I don't know who created this choral miracle, but the whole morning seemed lighter and brighter.

We run out of jeans, belts, socks and backpacks, but it is OK. The migrants are humming and singing throughout the morning. One elderly gentleman begins to sing alone, songs of love and pathos and longing. There are tears streaming down his face. He is back in his village singing to his wife, his children, his lost life.

Ultimately, these men will most likely do menial, backbreaking work and live in small crowded rooms. They will have dreams for their children, and for their children's children.

And I will remember them singing *Cielito Lindo* on a rainy day, with gusto and hope.

Samaritan Jaime and baby Angel.

CHAPTER FOUR

Autumn

To adapt an image from Carl Sandburg, autumn sneaks into the desert "on little cat feet." It is a subtle change of season here on the border. There is no dramatic conflagration of blazing crimson or gold leaves sweeping the landscape. Instead, autumn is difficult to detect, with subtle but increasing waves of beige, yellow and tan. The green grasses that flourished during the monsoon summer go to seed and die back for a winter's rest.

The desert meadows often look like fields of wheat. In fact, many are edible grains. Amaranth grows wild in the desert and is a unique plant with little white popcorn-like flowers cultivated by pre-Columbian Aztecs. Sunflowers along the roadside are ten feet tall, and the birds feast on the seeds before flying south to Mexico.

To me, autumn is the best season of the year everywhere. The days are mild, and the hot, humid monsoon weather of southern Arizona has passed.

Kitchen duty at the *comedor*

Here in the desert we all come out of hiding. We can sit outside again on the patio during the daylight hours without baking our feet on the tiles. The birds aren't panting at the birdbaths. We start hiking again, enjoying the canyons and *arroyos*.

A JOYFUL NOISE

Things begin to pick up again at the *comedor* as the weather is more hospitable to traveling. The numbers increase, but the stories remain tragically the same. There is despair and disappointment and injury. Heroic acts in the desert are also shared—there are stories of bravery about the Border Patrol, migrants and Samaritans. We are greeted on our walk to the *comedor* with cries of "We love you! You are all angels! Do you have any socks today?"

When I was a child growing up on Chicago's South Side, I attended the local Baptist church. My earliest memory of Sunday school was memorizing Psalm 100 from the Bible:

"Make a joyful noise unto the Lord, all ye lands."

As a small child the verse brought up visions of dancing, clanging cymbals, bells, singing and generally having a good time. I couldn't figure out why the Baptists didn't dance and their parties were such staid affairs. It was punch and cookies in the church basement. Dancing was forbidden by the local Baptist church. There were a lot of rules about what you could and could not do, and most of the rules seemed to land on the forbidden list. No dancing, no alcohol, no swearing.

Where was the joyful noise?

Perhaps it is no coincidence that I took up percussion in high school and still play timpani in a band today. I have always liked to bang on things. Music and celebration are an important part of my life. Sitting on hard pews listening to long sermons is not.

I can honestly say I do not remember one sermon from my years of churchgoing as a child or teenager. But I remember the singing, the choir anthems and especially the festive performances at Christmas and Easter. Singing in the choir was the lure that brought me to church each Sunday. The old hymns still make me misty when I sing them. And I continue to love the hundredth Psalm.

One morning our Samaritan group arrived a bit early at the *comedor* and breakfast had not yet been served. After a very personal and moving prayer by Father Martín speaking to the experience of migration and the separation from family and children, we all pitched in to help serve the group of migrants present that day.

Passing the steaming plates of scrambled eggs with chilies, onions and pork, pinto beans and a cheesy pasta, along with the hot coffee and *atole de canela* (a hot milk/cinnamon drink), the migrants once again bowed their heads with gratitude. Many wore rosaries and medals around their necks and had visible tattoos on arms and torsos.

―――

Suddenly the prevailing mood of solemnity changes. Sister Lorena, the nun in charge today, cranks up a boom box with some pretty wild salsa music and begins to dance up and down the crowded aisles. Heads are bobbing to the beat.

One of the kitchen ladies comes out of the tiny *cocina* (kitchen) and joins her in some amazing hip shimmies. Soon Shura, the Samaritan founder, is sashaying across the crowded room as well. It is hard to stand still. The beat is infectious. I want to join in but hold back out of shyness, trying to comprehend the incongruity of it all.

Impulsively, one of the younger migrants leaps up before finishing his breakfast, executes some complicated dance steps toward the front of the room, and begins twirling Shura around in a wild and raucous salsa, complete with dips and dizzying turns. It is spontaneous combustion. There is clapping and swaying and, yes, most definitely a joyful noise. This is religion in motion.

After the revelry of this breakfast dance, the young migrant who has performed his salsa of uninhibited joy tells me he is from Ocotlán, Jalisco, a city near Guadalajara. He is perhaps in his early twenties, and has not seen his mother in five years. His eyes, sparkling with energy during his impromptu dance, now suddenly become clouded and sad.

His hair is long and curly and fastened in a ponytail. I remark on his long hair, and he tells me he made a promise to God that he would not cut his hair until he sees his mother once again. She lives in San Francisco, California, and cannot visit him in Mexico due to "the laws of *Los Estados Unidos*." Our dancing friend is determined to cross the border and see his mother once more.

A Samaritan offers to call his mother and tell her about this young man's journey. We talk with him about the dangers of the desert and the long trek to California. He is adamant about this odyssey. He will attempt the journey. He reminds me of young men everywhere who do risky things and ignore the dangers and consequences.

I will not forget the dance of joy that emanated from this young man or his vow to see his mother again. Our dancing friend does not want to reside in the United States, nor does he want citizenship in the United States. He has no intention of staying in the United States. He has a life in Ocotlán, Mexico.

He wants to see his mother.

And I want desperately to fix this.

OF BURROS AND CHOCOLATE

I sat in a doctor's office recently half-listening to the TV, which was tuned to a politically conservative station. There is a lot of congressional debate going on these days (2012) about comprehensive immigration reform, and the Republicans and Democrats have their respective versions of what is best.

President Obama says immigration is a top priority of his second term of office. Flashing across the screen was a poll saying 68 percent of the people in the United States favor the Arizona anti-immigration bill and think that anyone in this country without proper documentation should be deported. Period. The remainder believe that comprehensive immigration reform is needed. Maybe 10 percent are simply undecided about the matter.

So 68 percent of Americans want to kick out the "illegals."

As I entered the exam room of my doctor, a Mexican-American man raised in a suburb of Laredo, Texas, I thought about his own success story as a busy medical specialist in the small border town of Nogales, Arizona. He is competent and gregarious and has asked me now and then about what it is I do at *el comedor* in Nogales, Sonora, just across the border. So today I asked him how he decided to become a doctor.

~~~

He was raised in a family of many children and not enough money. His schooling was mediocre at best. Working at a gas station throughout high school, he would do his homework in between gassing up the cars. His papers were always marked down because they were dirty and stained with oil and grease. This still rankles him. His math papers were perfect, but he was docked 10 percent because of the grease stains. The frustrations of thirty years ago are still right there on the surface as we talk.

He tells me about seeing migrants pass through their yard when he was a little boy. His mother would tell the weary travelers to drink from the garden hose and then would run inside to prepare food for them. And she would ask her son, about eight years old at the time, to take the food outside to the waiting migrants. My doctor speaks of how he hated this chore.

"There is not enough food to feed everyone in our own family! Why should we give these strangers our food when we don't have enough ourselves? I hate doing this!"

And his mother would put her hand on his head and quote an old Mexican proverb: "How can a burro know about fine chocolate, *mi hijito* (my little son)?"

How can a little boy so young really understand what is going on here? How can a little boy understand that when you see someone who is hungry and tired and thirsty, you give him water and food and a bit of shade? You share what you have. You help those in dire need.

She told him that someday he would understand.

My doctor tells me that it took him many years to understand. He points to a photo on the wall of his mother, a beautiful Mexican woman with a classic profile and long black hair. It is obvious to me that he reveres her as a saint. Recently he built a beautiful new office and clinic, and in the foyer is a plaque dedicating this building to his mother.

She taught him well the lessons of compassion and how we treat those in need. His skill as a doctor reflects the gentle spirit and tenderness of his mother. I'm lucky to have him as my doctor.

The laws and policies concerning immigration are wrong and inhumane, and they don't work. It is the burro trying to understand the nuances of fine chocolate. The answers are not simple. But this I know: The wall is one expensive boondoggle.

What is missing from the equation has to do with the compassion and kindness I have been taught to expect from the United States. We are better than these endless arguments about states' rights superseding federal law, or vice versa. We have somehow gotten on the wrong track here. It reminds me of a Thomas Aquinas essay I read in college about how many angels can dance on the head of a pin. It is an endless debate leading nowhere.

We are wasting time. People are dying, probably today, not far from my home. Mass migration has been happening for more than a decade among our neighbors to the south. Most of the migrants are not smugglers hauling a load of marijuana. The largest loads of the illicit drug trade come through the major ports of entry hidden in trucks. Not on the backs of immigrants.

Forget the wall. Try to understand the nuances of fine chocolate. Walls just make the problems worse. They keep undocumented people locked in the United States, and they keep people trapped in Mexico. Families remain separated, and this creates the tragedy each week that I visit the *comedor*.

It's all pretty basic, really. My mother taught me the same lessons as my good doctor's mother from Laredo taught him. Love your neighbor as yourself.

DIOS ESTÁ AQUÍ (GOD IS HERE)[14] —a popular Mexican song

Music is often played at the *comedor* and brings up strong emotions among the migrants and the aid workers, too. One day the Samaritans were waiting patiently with the pilgrims for breakfast to begin. Everyone was hungry, and the smells from the kitchen were making my stomach rumble. It was time to get the show on the road and pass out the food. Instead, Sister Lorena put a song on the boom box, and within two minutes most of the people in the room were weeping.

Trying my best to discern the lyrics, the Spanish words were not translating in my English-speaking brain. The song, "Dios Está Aquí (God Is Here)," a softly swinging tune, is popular in Mexico, and I watched as the desperate men and women silently mouthed the words, some singing along. The women passed around a roll of toilet tissue to wipe their tears. The men placed their hands over their eyes and faces. The Samaritans looked on, first in puzzlement and then compassion, as we slowly comprehended the lyrics and the feelings in the room.

The gentle message of the lyrics speaks of God being everywhere, in the air we breathe and the sunlight shining on our faces.

Sister Lorena gives several migrants the opportunity to express their thoughts after the song ends.

One woman observes, "If God is here, and I am here, I must have done something horribly wrong to suffer as I have these past weeks."

She goes on to say that God must not want to protect her or care for her. How could He allow horrible things to happen to her if He were indeed "here"? Lorena does her best to assure this broken woman that God loves her and that she has done nothing to deserve the abuse and horror of the past weeks.

But her question remains with me for hours. The migrants continually ask, "Why isn't God protecting us when all we want to do is work and see our families? We are not criminals. Our only crime is crossing a boundary and seeking work. We ask nothing but the chance to survive."

—◆—

I feel helpless in these situations. I looked at the throng of people at the *comedor*, all of them stripped of home and family, and wondered what could be done here to change this sad state of affairs. Is it true that the poor will always be among us?

As the morning progressed and I sat with the women, I realized that hearing their stories was all I could do today. Listening with as much attention and empathy as I could muster was what mattered at this moment. It was a time of simply loving my neighbors.

Thankfully, the beans and rice were plentiful on this morning, and soon there was more music playing on the

Flowers and festivities during *Día de los Muertos*

boom box. This time it was a popular folk song about traveling a long distance to find a lost love. The mood shifted, the
food was nourishing and the tears disappeared.

But the injustice of it all remained.

DÍA DE LOS MUERTOS

Early November brings a magical, colorful fiesta time to
Nogales, with feasting and music and marigolds. It is *Día de
los Muertos,* the Day of the Dead. The cemetery is around
the corner from the *comedor,* and the street is transformed
with souvenir venues, tents and musicians strumming their
guitars among the gravestones. Children are scrubbing the
graves and sweeping debris from the family plots. There are
bouquets of brightly colored marigolds for sale everywhere,

and the smell of *carne asada* (roasted beef) on the open fires and outdoor grills permeates the air.

I love contrasts and extremes, a hallmark of living in the Arizona desert. The blazing heat of the desert during the day and the forty-degree drop in temperature at night remind me that we're in a transition—winter is coming. The days are sunny, but at night you need a warm blanket.

Día de los Muertos is that kind of festival—a study of contrasts and extremes, a party of joy and sorrow, yin and yang. The Nogales cemetery, a place of sadness and grief, is today a place of singing and feasting. The streets are lined with booths selling bouquets of marigolds, candied sugar skulls and *pan dulce* (sweet breads). There are tiny, carefully crafted skulls of molded sugar, and children delight in carrying them through the streets.

Roasted beef on skewers slowly drips fat into the fires, and strolling guitarists and accordionists are everywhere. A man walks down the middle of the street holding a bunch of marigolds in one hand and a taco spilling over onto the sidewalk in the other. A couple of dogs follow him closely, licking up the juices from the *carne asada*.

Mexicans celebrate *Día de los Muertos* with a very different spirit from that of our American Hallowe'en. In Mexico, families gather around the graves of their departed loved ones, feast on favorite foods, pass around a bottle of tequila and spend the night singing and reminiscing about those who have died. They welcome the spirits of family and friends into their lives. It is a gentle, joyous and respectful sharing of feelings.

Nothing scary here. No ghosts or goblins or witches. Children help parents place marigolds in elaborate patterns on gravestones. The pungent fragrance of the golden flowers will help the spirits of the dead find their way to family and friends. Things are pretty upbeat in this old cemetery.

Our Samaritan group stops first at the *comedor*, where we see one hundred or more migrants lined up for breakfast. I meet Alberto, age twelve days. His proud papa holds him up for me to see. Alberto's mother is there as well and is glowing because her husband has just been released from a U.S. detention center. Papa is quietly weeping with happiness. His tears are unabashed and his emotions are for everyone to see. Alberto yawns and makes squeaky baby noises. Mama fusses over her newborn.

They have everything today. They have their baby and they are together. They are family.

"So where are you heading?" I ask this proud family.

They answer, "We will stay in Mexico until Alberto is stronger."

Wise parents. I rummage through the piles of clothing and find a classy Calvin Klein one-piece outfit for baby Alberto. There is hope in the eyes of this humble family. And they have nothing in the way of worldly goods. I see them stroll off toward the cemetery and the celebration.

Beginnings and endings—that is what this day is all about.

My Samaritan friends and I walk over to the festivities. I buy a sugar skull and a huge bouquet of marigolds and magenta cockscombs for decorating my own altar at home. We dine on the best *chile verde* (pork stew simmered with green chilies) I have had in years at a *taquería* along the street.

Afterward we walk through the U.S. Customs port of entry.

A Customs agent stops me, saying, "Hey, you cannot take the flowers with you!"

"But why?" I ask, holding my bouquet of marigolds.

"There are probably destructive insects on the flowers, and we don't want the infestation in the U.S.," he replies.

He looks sheepish as he orders me to hand over my bouquet of flowers. He is doing his job, following the rules. But I also sense that he doesn't want to follow these particular rules and would bend them if he could.

"What?" I protest. "The bugs don't know there is a border and a wall. They'll just fly over! How can you keep bugs in Mexico from flying into the U.S.?"

The Customs agent smiles, is actually quite cordial, and agrees. "I'm sorry," he says. "It's not me, it's the government. It's a rule."

Ah, yes, it's a rule. So I give him my beautiful marigolds. "Take these home to your own altar tonight," I tell him. "It is a tradition around here. It is *Día de los Muertos.*"

He smiles, takes my flowers and walks them over to the trash can.

As I watch the Customs agent dump my flowers, I ask him if he has ever celebrated *Día de los Muertos* in Nogales at the cemetery.

"Never been there," he answers.

Walking back to my car on the U.S. side, I can hear the singing and the gentle laughter across the wall that separates us from Mexico. The world seems saner over there today.

Viva Mexico!

Harry and baby Amor

MI AMOR (MY LOVE)

There are times when the actions of my migrant friends leave me speechless and upset for days. Especially when there are children sitting at the breakfast tables. An encounter with baby Amor and her grandmother is one I remember well.

~~~

Baby Amor (Spanish for *love*) is sitting at the breakfast table staring off into space as her grandmother tries to feed her the mashed pinto beans. The child never smiles, not once. All the cooing and jiggling and silly faces do not entice this baby to give us the tiniest grin.

Amor is eighteen months old, and she and her grandmother have just been released from a detention center. The child is from Sinaloa, heading to Utah with Grandma. They will try to cross again tonight even though the Border Patrol picked them up a few days ago in the desert. Dressed in a pink sleeper we have found in the donated bags of clothing, Amor looks spacey, sad and expressionless. Her skin is sallow and there is a rash on her baby cheeks.

Harry, a Samaritan colleague, bounces her around the room, hoping the movement will bring a giggle to this small child. There is nothing. No tears, no smiles. Just a look that seems to pass right through me.

Grandma knows the risks, yet is determined to try again. She lives in Utah, speaks both Spanish and English, and must bring little Amor to the United States for reasons she cannot discuss.

"You really don't want to know," she tells me. She is shaking her head and has the look of disappointment in her family and her circumstances. Grandma is on the run.

I ask if she has a plan after she crosses into the desert. She tells me her son will meet her.

"Everything will be OK. I have my cell phone." Grandma sounds determined and confident.

I, on the other hand, am aghast. Climbing over a fifteen-foot wall with a small child is beyond my comprehension.

"How did you happen to settle in Utah?"

This feisty grandma lights up and tells me she loves Utah, loves the people and is "almost a Mormon."

Amor quietly watches me talk. Her eyes look like they are a thousand years old. She is thin and appears to be six months old, not eighteen months. She does not try to walk or crawl and needs to be supported when she sits on the bench.

I tell them both that there is another meal at four that afternoon. Be sure to feed Amor and take extra nourishment. The nights are cold now. We have blankets. I show her the socks, the jackets. The Samaritans implore Grandma to spend some time in Nogales and wait in this place for a while. Perhaps her son can visit her here. Grandma shrugs off the advice and begins looking for warmer jackets, shoes that fit and some diapers.

If there are miracles afoot, tonight is the night that Amor and Grandma will need one. I think about Amor for weeks.

She and Grandma leave the *comedor*, and no one ever hears from them again.

SHOW ME YOUR PAPERS

Arizona is mired in the controversial anti-immigration law SB1070, with citizens polarized and passionate about the Latino community. The federal government relies on local law enforcement to identify and detain suspected illegal immigrants. Arizona law enforcement has a history of detaining nonviolent, low-risk immigrants who are then placed in the state's detention system, often for months. Through contracts with private prisons and county jails, ICE detains three thousand immigrants on any given day in Arizona.[15]

In 2009, President Obama announced plans to overhaul immigration policies in an effort to improve detention-center management and to stop picking up immigrants with minor infractions or no criminal history. To date, reforms have resulted in little or no change in the five detention centers in Arizona.[16]

A large number of migrants I meet each week have been in a detention center for weeks, sometimes for months. If they were picked up during the summer months and placed in a detention center, they are often released several months later in winter and appear at the *comedor* in a T-shirt and ragged pants. They have no jackets or other warm clothing for the colder months.

Temperatures are in the forties in the morning, and I find migrants shivering in front of the shelter, hoping that the Samaritans have jackets and warm hats to dispense. To make matters even more deplorable, migrants are often deported in the middle of the night on the streets of Nogales, Mexico. I am told that this is a psychological ploy that will discourage future crossings. Sometimes when approaching the *comedor*, we will see men and women hud-dled, crouching on the sidewalk, trying to stay warm in the chill autumn air.

Border Patrol agents at the Nogales station informed me that they can hold an undocumented person for only twelve hours. Hence, if a person is picked up at 2 p.m., he might be deported and left on the streets of Nogales at 2 a.m.

My Samaritan colleagues hand out blankets to the newly deported so they have some warmth while they wait for the *comedor* to open its doors for breakfast. I remember meeting one man who ripped off his shirt, which had been issued by the detention center, in spite of the cold morning temperatures. He did not want to wear the garment one more minute. I rummaged through a bag of clothing looking for a shirt and jacket for this fellow. He was weeping as he said he would rather freeze than wear the jail shirt.

─*www*─

One week I notice a man looking for a warm jacket and clean socks. His name is Juan, and he has been in a detention center off and on for the past four years. Juan speaks perfect English. He has lived in Houston since he was four years old and now has a wife and three children.

So I ask, "Why have you been locked up for three years?"

"Well, I did some stupid things when I was young," is his reply.

"Like what?"

"When I was sixteen years old, I was caught speeding without a license. So I went to traffic school, got my license suspended for a while. Thank God I didn't hit anyone. I was just a stupid teenager."

I am puzzled about this story. "Why were you picked up and locked in detention? Surely something you did eleven years ago doesn't mean you go to detention for three years, does it?"

Juan's eyes well up. He clutches his jacket and a plastic grocery sack holding his belongings. Just thinking about his jail time upsets him. "I have tried to get back home to Houston many times," he tells me. "I get picked up by the Border Patrol, put in a detention center, get deported, and then I try and cross again. Now I am considered a criminal. I have been fighting this for three years."

Juan is agitated telling me his story. He paces in the aisles.

"I've made appeals to the judge. Finally I just signed some papers when they promised to let me go. But I am being deported to Guatemala, where I was born. Guatemala! I have no family there. I know no one. The papers I signed say I cannot return to Houston, ever."

If a person is not a Mexican citizen, Mexico returns the migrant to the country of origin.

Juan is a professional photographer in Houston, specializing in weddings, *quinceañeras* and parties. ICE picked him up four years ago, and he is not sure why—maybe an old parking ticket. But when his records were checked, law enforcement found the old driving violation from when he was sixteen. Next thing he knew, he was in a detention center in Livingston, Texas.

"What was it like being in a detention center in Texas?" I ask.

Juan sits down. He is clearly upset talking about it. I back off. He abruptly asks me to take his photograph in front of the *Virgen de Guadalupe*. He breathes deeply, regaining some composure. Juan is shaken by the memories, and I feel like I have invaded some sacred space. I have overstepped a boundary with this man. He poses in front of the mural of the *Virgen,* clutching his jacket and his plastic sack. He's managed to find a decent pair of shoes that fit. I take a couple of pictures.

"I was locked up in this room with other beds and a big glass window between the rooms, with more beds. And more rooms. There were no windows to the outside to let in light. In fact, they never turned off the lights, so there was never any darkness. I was only let out of the room one hour a day, and never outside. I did not see the sun for weeks."

I ask about any physical abuse. He just shrugs.

And then he says the most amazing thing of all: "I don't blame your country for this. You can't just let everyone across the border. But your country is going to extremes! This is crazy. I have a job, and I've lived in Houston almost my whole life!"

I could not look him in the eye at that moment. Of course, I cannot verify the accuracy of his story. Maybe there was some criminal record in his past. And maybe not.

One thing is certain. Juan will not be heading to Guatemala. He is heading home to Houston for Christmas.

"I have got to be home with my kids at Christmas. I will travel alone. I know the way. I've done it before."

I advise Juan that if he gets picked up, it will mean more detention, more lockup time. I give him the phone number of a U.S. attorney who may be able to help him if he is picked up during his trek to Houston.

He gives me a hug, crosses himself and steps out into the sun.

And I feel utterly helpless as I watch him go.

Since my encounter with Juan, the Supreme Court has struck down three out of four provisions in Arizona's controversial SB1070, the anti-immigration law. The court upheld the "show me your papers" provision, which requires Arizona law enforcement to stop and detain any individual without warrant on the sole basis of "reasonable suspicion" regarding his immigration status. Also, President Obama has announced that immigrants under thirty years of age who arrived here as children and have stayed in school and kept out of trouble will not be detained and deported as illegal immigrants.

I do hope that Juan is safe and with family. I am saddened he spent three years in a detention center for the crime of trying to get home to his family and his job in Houston.

Migrants tell me of being locked up in detention centers in Arizona, California and Texas. Many of them are women who have no idea where their children are and have limited access to telephones and attorneys. I talk with family members in Nogales who are trying without success to find a spouse or a son imprisoned in a detention center in Arizona or Texas.

Samaritans often assist in such searches, but it is not easy to penetrate the bureaucratic wall of the prison system. The largest migrant detention facility in the country is located in Florence, Arizona, and is a part of the Corrections Corporation of America (CCA), a private for-profit company that builds and staffs prisons. There are 2,300 beds in this detention center. The prison makes money if the beds are filled. Hence, the more migrants locked up in detention, the more profits for CCA. Sadly, these prisons are a growth industry in Arizona.

When I talk with deported migrants, they have the demeanor of a traumatized person. They are reticent to talk about their experience, and there is a lack of trust and candor in their remarks. Women especially give me little or no eye contact. They look frightened and beaten down emotionally. I suspect there has been abuse and assault during their detention. Their heads are bowed, and most just want to go back to their home village somewhere in Mexico.

The most heartbreaking situations are those of migrants who have children in the United States and cannot return to their families. Often their children are American, born in the U.S.A. In the documentary film *Lost in Detention*,[17] several women were interviewed regarding rape by male and female staff during their imprisonment. The women had no recourse for these atrocities. They just wanted to get out of prison and decided that keeping their mouths shut about the assaults was the best way to be released. Many prayed that they would be deported to Mexico, just to get out of the detention center.

I have a relationship with a woman who has several children in Phoenix but has been deported to Nogales, Mexico. She is an undocumented worker and has lived in the United States for fifteen years. She rarely sees her children in Phoenix. I don't know why she was deported, but I have seen her around the *comedor* for a year or more. She works as a driver of a van for one of the Mexican immigration services and often transports migrants to the *comedor* in the morning.

She became pregnant, and my personal belief is that she was creating another family in Nogales because she sees very little hope of returning to her home in Phoenix. She is thirty years old. A strong survivor, she is doing what she can to make her life bearable in Nogales.

Her baby was born during the hot summer months, and this woman brought her infant to the *comedor* for our admiration and approval. The new baby girl is dressed in red and white and is all ruffles and pink skin.

The ability to cope with impossible situations, such as separation from children and family, both astounds and humbles me as I stand in the presence of such resilient people. It also infuriates me, as there is no reason for such inhumane policies.

Wives separated from husbands, children separated from parents—this is a common thread in the migrant's life. Is it not enough that people are fleeing their homeland due to economic conditions and violence from drug trafficking? Yet on top of that, if caught by U.S. immigration authorities, they will be separated from their families.

Hunger, poverty, and reunification with family are, however, strong motivating forces. Crossing the desert and risking death seems like the only option. Thousands take that risk.

During my time at the *comedor*, I get only part of the story from these weary travelers. The shelter is a place of transience. People do not stay here week after week. An average stay is three days, and then they are gone.

I have met many people living the life of a nomad. They work in *Los Estados Unidos* in the orchards or the fields or at a restaurant somewhere in Florida and then migrate back home to Chiapas or Guerrero, perhaps being picked up by ICE or the Border Patrol and spending time in a detention center before moving onward again.

Like birds, they are constantly migrating. This is their life. Many of the older migrants have made the journey into the United States a dozen, maybe two dozen times. They have lost count. South to north, north to south. Following the harvest, following their hearts.

There is a determination and sense of sacrifice here that is difficult to describe. Why do these people keep traveling back and forth?

This is what they tell me: They do this to protect their families from violence, to provide food for their loved ones, to send their children to good schools. Traveling back and forth has become the rhythm of their life.

Always there is the nagging conviction that something better lies down the road and over the wall. Globalization has created inequities in the economy and food distribution. At two thousand miles, the U.S. border with Mexico is the longest geographical boundary between a technologically advanced nation and an emerging industrialized country. Conflicts and intense emotions emerge when the "haves" watch the "have-nots" crossing the line and climbing the wall.

We have a lot of creature comforts in the United States that Mexicans want. Many items in Mexico are more expensive than in the United States, including food, appliances, autos and computers. In a report from 2011, the Organization for Economic Cooperation and Development says Mexico has the world's second-highest income disparity between the rich and the poor. The United States is number four.[18]

Strolling the streets of downtown Nogales, Mexico, sometimes I see small children peering through the metal slats of the wall, looking with curiosity at a place where they cannot go. They are looking at the people in the United States. I wonder what is going through their little minds. Many of the children know they will probably never cross to the other side of the fence. They are simply too poor or they have no vision of another kind of life.

Once when I was crossing through customs from Mexico into the United States, there was a Latina girl, probably twelve years old, in front of me with her aunt. When the young girl presented her passport, there was a long pause as the official stared at his computer screen. The girl was asked to leave the line and was briskly escorted by a U.S. marshal into a nearby room. The girl looked around in confusion as the agent took her by the elbow and firmly guided her into a room and closed the door.

The aunt cried out, "What is going on? Where are you taking her?"

A U.S. Customs agent involved in the process excitedly pumped his arm and danced around like he had just made a touchdown, shouting, "Yes!"

Another agent said, "This must be your first, eh?"

It was his first catch; he had caught a twelve-year-old girl. There were a couple of high-fives all around. It was muted jubilation at the border crossing. Someone waiting in line with me suggested that maybe the child had a phony passport.

I felt like a coward watching this spectacle.

The girl looked terrified. The aunt was removed from the line and escorted to the side of the customs passageway.

Those of us who witnessed this event looked on, trying to comprehend what had just transpired. When I reached the Customs agent with my passport, I asked him why they'd removed the little girl.

"Is she OK?" I asked. The agent said this was a routine check. "Everything is under control. Next!"

Everything is *not* under control. My mind was out of control.

A little Mexican girl looked confused and afraid and was separated from her adult companion by uniformed men with guns. I saw it happen less than ten feet from where I stood.

I have no idea what the real story is behind this incident, but it didn't feel like America. It didn't look like a welcoming committee. It looked like something out of Kafka. I felt complicit in the drama. I still think about that little girl and hope she is safe and in school and will someday do brilliant things. I am sure she will never forget this incident.

COMEDOR FASHION

Each week I bring a few bags of used clothing, shoes and backpacks to the *comedor* to help the travelers who arrive in torn and ragged pants. Shoes, belts and clean socks are especially appreciated. The discrepancy between the rich and the poor is clearly evident when the Samaritans unpack the sacks and take a look at some of the labels. We see Patagonia, GAP, Eddie Bauer and Banana Republic outdoor gear. They're all there.

For the ladies, stylish fashion labels from New York

occasionally make an appearance. One week there were custom-sewn men's shirts from Italy. Many of the items still have tags on them; they have never been worn. Our throwaways are some of the best clothes and shoes that many of the migrants have ever worn.

The ladies love the jeans with the studs and sequins. The men look for Levis and a packet with a razor blade and a toothbrush. They all stand a bit taller looking over the clean clothes, and there is joking in the room about the large sizes of so many American men and women compared with the smaller stature of the Latinos.

Belts are very popular and necessary to hold up the large-size pants. There is something about new clothes that just makes a body feel better. It's a bit like Christmas, at least for that moment.

The sisters, the Samaritans and a couple of high school students help organize the clothes onto tables for the men, women and children. The migrants come into the shelter in small groups and pick out the clothes needed for the days ahead. At first there is silence and no one speaks. But then things pick up a bit.

Someone finds a pair of jeans that fits perfectly and a fleecy hooded jacket for the cold autumn nights. One guy dances around holding up some Calvin Klein boxer shorts. A young woman admires a "Life is good" T-shirt and models it for others.

Life is good? There is always a little irony in spite of the hard times.

Occasionally the outfits we display for distribution are ridiculous. A flimsy negligee, a wool pinstripe suit appropriate for Wall Street or a satin evening gown is unpacked for our inspection, and the aid workers have great laughs. Often Shura will try one on and parade about the *comedor* modeling the outrageous costumes. Migrants shake their heads in puzzled and amused laughter, wondering what goes on with these crazy Americans.

The migrants have true grit. They are tough and unstoppable. Of course, the biggest obstacles are the U.S. immigration authorities and law enforcement. But the pilgrims shrug, and figure out how to jump that wall anyway. There are no slackers at the *comedor*.

The Virgin in the snow

CHAPTER FIVE

Winter

LA POSADA

I figured things would slow down in December when the Christmas holidays arrived, casting their special magic on both sides of the border. I was wrong. The migrants arrived in droves, leaving the United States and preparing to journey to their homes in Mexico and Central America. Many used the shelter as a stopover before heading back farther south. Most would remain in Mexico for a month or more.

Christmas in Mexico is a religious celebration centered on family and a special tradition, *la posada*, the search for the inn and shelter. Migrants living and working in the United States travel to their villages in Mexico to spend time with their families and celebrate the birth of Christ. Gift-giving is not at the center of the Christmas holiday in Mexico. Rather, it is a time for family and a break from months of hard work in the fields and orchards of *Los Estados Unidos.*

I have heard about *la posada* all my life—a Christmas procession reenacted in Mexico with a pregnant Mary and a troubled Joseph searching for a place to rest and being turned away in Bethlehem. After days of searching, they find a humble stable because there is no room at the inn. Mary gives birth to the baby Jesus among the animals on a bed of straw. It is a poignant and troubling tale, difficult to ponder two thousand years later.

Throughout Mexico there are *posadas* in cities and villages. I was very excited about an invitation from Fathers Martín and Francisco to join in a *posada* in Nogales. The story of the birth of Christ has always touched my heart. The narrative has lasted more than two thousand years, bringing up all kinds of emotions about babies, birth, the desert, poverty. All of it has affected me in ways I truly do not understand.

It is early December and the day is bright and sunny and crisp; our little group of Samaritans is on the downtown plaza of Nogales preparing for a parade through the city. Migrants, local Mexican citizens, Arizonans, teenagers from a local high school, musicians—we all line up with banners and a sense of curiosity, not knowing what to expect.

"Mary," a local high school student, climbs onto a waiting burro with the help of "Joseph" and a glittering angel, complete with halo. They are María and José. It is a two thousand-year-old tableau coming to life on the streets of Nogales. The *farmacias* are still hawking Viagra, and the liquor stores are still doing a bustling business, but there we are, queued up with a donkey and the Holy Family.

The banners we carry are blatantly outspoken and strongly political:

- "The laws are unjust when they separate families"
- "We must reform the immigration system so there is no separation of families"

The message on our placards is direct and courageous. The time has come for change, and the time is now.

We slowly walk through the streets of Nogales toward the *comedor*, which is two miles away. People stop and watch as we stroll through the neighborhoods. Some wave, and many pause and say a short prayer. The donkey wants to nip everyone who gets within arm's length, and María looks beatific through it all. The angel's halo is askew, and some women help her adjust her wings and sparkling headpiece.

And it is somewhere in the middle of this humble parade that I realize that the Holy Family mirrors the migrants walking with me on this December afternoon.

María and José were not welcome in Bethlehem and were not given a room in which to stay for the night. There was no room at the inn, as this was the time of the census, when many travelers were seeking shelter in Bethlehem. Doors were closed to the couple even though María was obviously going to have a baby very soon.

Soon after the birth, the family was forced to flee to another country, Egypt, to save the life of their newborn son. They were on the run, and all they really wanted was a place to call home and to be together as a family.

Just like the migrants who surround me in this *posada*.

I'd never made that connection before. Christmas and the birth of Jesus are about a family trying to stay together in a safe place. It is about injustices provoked by governmental systems that do not honor the fundamental importance of a family staying together. It is about oppressive treatment of the poor.

It is about us, today, in this place.

Our *posada* stops three times along the two-mile walk back to the *comedor*, and each time a deported person speaks of a desire to return to family and home. He or she speaks of spending months in detention centers in the United States while struggling to find family members. I hear their stories of being near death after days in the desert.

During the long walk, popular music plays from speakers on a pickup truck. The music is all related to immigration and searching for home. It seems incongruous at first, hearing the popular tunes blaring out of the loudspeakers, but it also adds a bit of fun to our parade. Our little group dances and sways to the music as we slowly make our way back to the *comedor*.

I find myself carefully stepping around potholes and dog poop as we wend our way through the Nogales neighborhoods. I walk with migrants, I walk with prosperous Nogales businessmen, I walk with tears in my eyes.

Women sing as our procession slowly makes its way. The lyrics are brave and the women sing out with vigor and attitude:

> *You were also a migrant,*
> *You came from another place.*
> *You had no papers*
> *You must remember that.*

Not only is this a religious celebration of the story of

The *posada* procession through Nogales beside the wall

Christmas, but also it is a strong political statement to everyone who watches as we slowly walk through this border city. It is a solemn procession. At times it is jubilant, as people on the streets cheer when we walk by their shops and homes. Children wave balloons. I observe shopkeepers crossing themselves, stopping their activities as they step outside to watch us walk by.

And then we finally arrive at our destination. The women of the church have prepared a feast for everyone in the *posada,* and the *comedor* is decorated for a party. The burro carrying María is ready for a flake of hay. This is definitely a very Mexican party, and we are the delighted guests.

Somehow there is room for all of us and plenty of food. We are offered a delicious hot punch of fruit juices, and plates are piled with stewed chicken, potatoes, beans and a pasta dish. The salsa could have started a bonfire and warms us up as we crowd around tables in the chill of the evening. Chocolate cupcakes are passed among the guests, and we are pleasantly full of good food and good cheer.

And here is the reality: A two thousand-year-old story is as relevant today as it was so long ago. The borders of Pakistan and Afghanistan, Palestine and Israel, North Korea and South Korea, and Mexico and the United States create havoc in people's lives. Families fall apart. Women and children suffer. No one wins.

These are the things I ponder on the long walk back to *Los Estados Unidos* and my own waiting family. I walk freely from one side of the border to the other with my passport, my ticket to freedom. My migrant friends watch me as I walk through customs to the other side of the wall.

THE FROST IS ON THE PUMPKIN

December in Arizona is full of surprises. I have basked in the sun on the patio of my home at noon and awakened to a dusting of snow the next morning. On one such morning, I hurriedly scraped the ice and snow from my car, pulled some fleece vests and sweaters out of my closet for donations at the *comedor* and headed to Mexico.

Wondering if anyone had been caught in the night's freezing temperatures in the desert, I tried to visualize what it must be like trekking across the desert toward a dream of American prosperity. The wind was razor-sharp and penetrated my layers of fleece. For the first time this winter, I needed warm gloves.

Many times I have seen the migrants at the *comedor* looking at newspaper ads of Americans in shiny kitchens eating mountains of holiday food. A gleaming car sits in front of the suburban home, and children happily play on the swing set. These Norman Rockwell scenes play heavily in migrants' decisions to leave home and provide creature comforts for their families.

I pictured them huddled in some cave in the desert trying to stay warm during this unexpected cold snap, imagining a home in America with a fancy stove, a crackling fire in the fireplace and a pantry full of food.

On this particular snowy day, our group of Samaritans walks into Mexico bearing gifts of Christmas cards and cookies for our migrant friends and the *comedor* staff. While sifting through the bags of clothing and shoes, Shura, an uninhibited prankster, finds a red velvet teddy, a sexy little lingerie number that a Tucson friend has decided to donate to the cause. She quickly puts it on over her jeans and stops traffic on our walk to Mexico. The truckers, the tourists, everyone

A Christmas gift for Sergio

honks and shouts and hoots at Shura, who struts her stuff on the way to the shelter.

Privately, I stew because the priests and the nuns at the *comedor* might not approve of such outlandish behavior.

I am wrong.

They all pose for photos with the stylish Shura, and, of course, the migrants just shake their heads with laughter and disbelief at the crazy Americans. There is so little to laugh about in these situations that we milk every moment that arises. It is a time of merriment and tomfoolery. It is sexy Shura modeling some outrageous Christmas lingerie on a cold December day among a hundred lost refugees.

We are laden with bags of cookies, Christmas cards and good cheer this week. The peddlers, the newspaper sellers, the windshield washers trying to make a few pesos at the border all descend on our group when they see us parading through Homeland Security and the Mexican Customs offices. There are hugs and high-fives as we hand out the cards and cookies.

Approaching the *comedor*, we see Sergio, the homeless man who had survived severe acid burns six months ago. Standing on the curb in his ragged pants and hoodie, Shura gives him a special card and a bag of cookies.

Sergio is puzzled and hands the card back to Shura. It becomes clear to us that he has never received a Christmas card, and doesn't know quite what to make of all this. We put a five-dollar bill in his glittery Christmas card, and Sergio looks hesitant and maybe a bit afraid during our gift-giving ritual. He has the look of a person who has no idea what this gesture is all about. It is almost as if he feels we are setting him up for ridicule, or worse.

Sergio quickly takes the five-dollar bill out of the envelope and then gives the card back to Shura. He isn't sure about the cookies, either. No explanation on our part will persuade him. The idea of receiving a gift is out of his realm of understanding. I think about that image—Sergio giving back the Christmas card and Shura trying to talk him into keeping the gift.

Finally he picks up the ragged little cardboard suitcase that he hauls everywhere and heads up the street.

It is one of those moments when we don't know quite what to do. This business of gift-giving and reaching out can be complicated and confusing. But we head on into the *comedor,* where the pilgrims are finishing their breakfast.

The place feels like a busy bus station. People are coming, people are going. Some are heading back to their villages for the Christmas season, and some are trying to cross into the United States. The mood is upbeat, and Shura's red velvet teddy outfit has brought a smile to everyone.

WE'RE SINGIN' IN THE RAIN

Winter in the Sonoran Desert can mean chilly rains and flooded streets. On one of our walks to the *comedor,* the heavens let loose with a deluge worthy of a scene in the movie *Singin' in the Rain.*

You remember. Gene Kelly is ankle-deep in water and dancing around a lamppost. As the heavens opened up on our band of Samaritans, we were indomitable, trudging through muddy rivers of water on the streets and dodging huge cranes that continued to build the wall. I waved at a wall-builder in a yellow slicker, and he waved back. We both looked at the sky and laughed at the deluge. The rainwater was rushing over the tops of my tennis shoes.

But we kept on going.

It is early December, and we are all carrying Christmas cookies and cards that we intend to give to the street peddlers, the windshield washers, the migrants, the priests, the nuns, the volunteers. But this is one serious rain, and we are the only people walking the streets. Peddlers have stayed home today.

Arriving at the *comedor*, we are greeted by at least seventy-five people crowded into the tiny space. Rain pelting loudly on the tin roof makes it impossible to communicate. We hurriedly unload a van that has transported our donated clothing and medical supplies.

We are soaked. The cookies are soggy; the cards are crumpled. Our Christmas gifts will have to wait until next week when the sun shines.

Buckets are strategically placed here and there, catching the rain pouring through gaps in the metal roof. And then I spy the simple colorful Christmas lights and decorations strung around the ceiling. The rains are literally washing away the hillside surrounding the shelter, but there is a warmth and cheeriness as we huddle inside against the storm. Even the *Virgen de Guadalupe* painting on the wall half-hidden behind the refrigerator is strung with Christmas lights, while paper roses and sacks of onions and potatoes sit at her feet.

I just stand in the middle of it all, so glad I am here, shivering, wet and happy.

There is quiet despair among the migrants today. They crowd closely together with makeshift trash bags draped over their heads. This is their rain gear, which is meager but better than nothing. Some wear plastic bags over their feet to keep them dry. The migrants gaze blankly into space, and I wonder where they will go for the rest of the day.

One young man is weeping uncontrollably. He is four-teen years old and has traveled from Honduras. A Samari-tan volunteer speaks softly to him and hugs his shoulder. I sit down and offer him my crumpled bag of cookies. Two other Hondurans tell me they will watch out for him. The young man tries to speak but cannot talk through his emo-tions. We, too, are speechless and can do nothing but offer our silent support.

Three women from Guerrero look at us quietly. They have been traveling for a month and are shivering under their colorful ponchos. One woman finds an ankle-length black wool coat, smiles and gives me a thumbs-up. The coat has an expensive New York label, and the woman looks stunning in it as she huddles quietly on a bench.

I sit with them and tell them in my simple, halting Span-ish that I wish them a safe journey. I'm not sure they under-stand what I'm saying, but they nod to me in gratitude. I open my backpack and dig out more cookies. We sit there, the four or us, munching on the cookies. We lean into each other for warmth on the long bench and listen to the pelt-ing of the rain outside.

The *comedor* smells faintly of mold and damp wool. The resident orange kitty comes around and licks up the crumbs falling to the floor.

I do not want to leave. I feel that there are times when the Samaritans receive much more than we give. Today is one of those times. We witness the human spirit in its struggle to survive with dignity and grace. Being here is a blessing. I will not forget this day. The place is full of Christmas spirit.

—-mm-—

Walking back across the border to my car, I stop at a coffee shop for lunch and some hot coffee on this wet day of drizzle. It is my birthday, and I have nothing planned.

Feeling sorry for myself, I watch a large extended family gather around three tables pushed together to accommodate their numbers. The family is Mexican American, and they are celebrating the Christmas season together, ordering piles of waffles topped with strawberries and whipped cream.

I desperately miss my own family. My kids are far-flung and hundreds of miles away. I wonder if they will call me. Will they remember that today is my birthday? Feeling like a child, I sit and watch all the confusion and happy revelry of the family in the restaurant. Six conversations at once. Children crawling under the tables. I envy their connection with each other. I want that connection with my own family today.

Pondering my morning with the displaced and distraught migrants at the *comedor*, I have a tiny glimmer of that feeling of aloneness when you are separated from those you love.

I am drowning in self-pity here in the coffee shop, but three women from Guerrero with whom I shared cookies a short while ago taught me to grab on to each moment and savor it for what it is. They had each other on this gray day but a very uncertain future. I am having a moment of warmth and a vicarious bonding with a happy family who were strangers to me, and I enjoy watching them share a boisterous lunch in this warm, cheery coffee shop.

My life is secure and comfortable. I have a husband who loves me and children who are doing well, though they live in far-off places. It is good to be alive on this day. It is okay to feel nostalgic and sad. In terms of the big picture, my situation is a thousand times safer than that of my migrant friends sitting a mile from me across the border. I feel the bittersweet emotions of this holiday season, that sad and happy mélange that overwhelms so many.

My kids call later in the evening. Such good kids.

I visualize the migrant woman in the long wool coat with the New York label, trudging across the desert tonight in the December drizzle. I light a candle for her when I get home.

BEARING GIFTS, WE TRAVERSE AFAR

On Christmas morning I put on my red Samaritan sweat-shirt with the hood and headed toward the border along with eight other Samaritans. We were a merry band of die-hard do-gooders on this sunny morn, and for once the bor-der crossing was deserted of people and vehicles. Most people were at home enjoying the revelry of brightly wrapped presents, excited children and good times around the Christmas tree.

A few Border Patrol agents were casually milling around the checkpoint, their weaponry reflected in the sun. We waved and shouted a greeting.

Approaching the *comedor* this Christmas Day was a dif-ferent story. The shelter was overflowing with pilgrims. Over the course of the next hour we were busy serving 150 migrants a breakfast of *menudo* (a hearty traditional Mexi-can soup) and bread. Everyone got a plastic bag of lunch

The *comedor* cat in the manger

treats today—fruit, a sandwich, some candies. I helped serve the hungry migrants, washed a hundred glasses, and then served more migrants and washed the dishes again. It felt good to be doing something on this special morning.

Shura was once again decked out in her bright red velvet Christmas lingerie, wearing this bit of nonsensical seasonal confection over her jeans and jacket. Her husband, Rich, sported a Christmas-elf hat that lighted up and played a silly song. The migrants applauded our little show of jollity as we entered the shelter, and for a moment there was a festive rhythm to the busy morning. Father Sean gave a Christmas blessing, and the multitude was fed.

The crèche in the corner was aglow with tiny lights, and everything was in place in the traditional stable—the manger, the angels, and all the animals. Mary and Joseph were on hand, too, but there was no baby Jesus just yet. The manger was empty save for the resident cat, which was curled up next to a cow and a camel. The cat knew the warmest place in the *comedor*, and he slept soundly under the Christmas lights on his bed of wood shavings with his head on the manger. Several migrants paused at the nativity scene, kneeling and bowing their heads.

—ww—

As breakfast ends, a migrant approaches me with his empty soup bowl, not sure where to line up with his dirty dishes. His face is heavily lined with dust and fatigue, and his eyes glitter with a wetness—from the cold, from pain, from tears? I do not know what is happening with this gentleman.

He wears a dirty khaki jacket, his shoes are muddy and worn through at the soles and his jeans are ripped. I can see my red sweatshirt reflected in his teary eyes. His eyes look red, too; then they look like all the reflected colors of the Christmas lights in the manger scene. I cannot see his irises, only the lights of the room reflected through his tears. His eyes are barely open as they lock onto mine, and we both look at each other awkwardly.

I ask him where he lives in Mexico.

"San Luis Potosí," is his reply, a city in the central part of Mexico. He is more than a thousand miles from home.

He goes on to explain that he has walked in the desert in the United States for nine days. He slept in the Nogales cemetery on Christmas Eve and is still very cold after a night of freezing temperatures.

I ask if he is hurt. He doesn't answer. When I ask if he is OK, he stares at the floor and just shakes his head back and forth. We stand there for what seems like an eternity, and I have a thousand questions I want to ask him, but my inadequate Spanish vocabulary cannot come up with the words. He looks so beaten and despairing that I am immobilized. In fact, there are no words in either English or Spanish that wouldn't seem contrived and superficial.

So there we stand, our masks removed, truthfully and transparently trying to make a human connection. I cannot get past his eyes; they are full of tears, and yet they do not spill over down his worn, weary face.

And I wonder on this Christmas morning how we can celebrate the birth of Jesus when God doesn't help this man through perhaps the lowest point in his life. His world is chaos, and I am having trouble entering his world and being with him. I realize that no matter what I say to this man, it will fall short.

The room is full of a hundred more stories as sorrowful and dramatic as this man's. It is overwhelming, and I wonder what I am doing here on this traditional morning of Christmas joy.

So, not knowing what to do, I take his empty soup bowl. It is a gesture of busy-ness, of trying to fill the self-conscious moment. He puts his hand on my shoulder and quietly says "*Gracias.*" I beseech him to be careful. I tell him I will say a prayer for his safety.

"*Feliz Navidad,*" I call after him. And he disappears out

the door. I wonder if I really know how to pray for anything, much less the man in the dirty khaki jacket.

—*—

After serving breakfast and distributing the clothes to the traveling pilgrims, one of the sisters asked our group of Samaritans if we would like to stay and witness the placing of the baby Jesus in the manger. The manger had been empty for weeks, and now it was Christmas Day and time for Jesus to sleep in his manger of straw.

And so we did. A lovely pageant of Christmas unfolded before our group. We watched two young women place the little statue of the infant Jesus in a small dish towel and swing the baby like a hammock, to and fro, while a group of migrants, sisters and kitchen helpers sang a song about the Christmas story (a very long song).

Then the baby Jesus was placed on a kitchen tray filled with candy and was slowly passed around the group. We were told that this was a time to ask Jesus for our own personal Christmas miracle, and take a piece of candy, a gift of His love. Each person was invited to kiss the infant statue and whisper a Christmas wish as the tray was passed around the circle.

Our group of Samaritans—this motley crew of Christians, Jews, Buddhists, agnostics, atheists and all the in-betweens—all stood there nervously and watched as the ritual evolved. It was a sweet moment of vulnerability for all of us, as we entered the tableau and each planted a kiss on the little Jesus statue. We bent down to whisper whatever we wished—our prayer for ourselves, our family, a sick friend or the world of pain we had just witnessed with the traumatized migrants. The question of whether we believe the story of Christmas didn't matter. It was a powerful moment for each of us.

It occurred to me at that moment, as I kissed the baby Jesus's forehead, how vulnerable a newborn baby is and how vulnerable I was that day in the presence of the suffering and despair of the migrants. I thought about my own children's infancies—their illnesses, their traumas, their defenseless nakedness.

My emotions were right on the surface.

Perhaps His message isn't experienced in our strongest moments but rather in our honest weakness. I have never found it easy to be with people who are suffering. I do not want to enter the chaos. And yet on this day I forgot about myself and my own discomfort and simply stood with a man who had been living a horrific drama, connecting as best I could. Being in his presence was a profound gift to me in ways I haven't quite figured out.

Our group was oddly quiet walking back to our waiting cars in the United States. I believe that God was with us in the unpretentious, simple surroundings of the *comedor* that day. I smile when I picture each individual bending over the little statue of Jesus on the bed of candy and whispering hopes for the future.

And that was the best Christmas gift of all.

HOPE IN THE NEW YEAR

The Samaritans gather these wintry Tuesday mornings in a

small deli in Tubac, Arizona, before heading down to Nogales and the challenges of the *comedor*. The deli personnel know us well. So do many of the customers, and they give us wide berth. The talk is spirited and loud, fueled by the caffeine and sugary pastries.

On this particular morning I checked in and out of three different conversations in the space of five minutes. Several tables were shoved together, as there were thirteen of us, with several visitors from Idaho and Wisconsin. A pair of teenagers were among the group, and there was some anticipation and nervousness about the whole venture. I told the teens that they might see young people their own age who have been walking or hopping trains for thousands of miles. After priming ourselves with coffee and tales of past trips to Nogales, we headed out the door.

The construction area for the wall that divides Mexico from the U.S.A was a beehive of machinery, dust and men shouting out orders. Someone commented that the wall might be a futile attempt at security, but at least it was putting a lot of people to work on our side of the border. On the Mexican side of the line, one fellow trying to sell his wares had a fever. It was January, and everyone seemed to have a cold. I promised to bring him some aspirin for his fever and discomfort on the trip back.

Arriving at the *comedor*, we saw the lineup of migrants outside the door, perhaps eighty, maybe more. Breakfast had already been served and they were waiting for us with our donations of clothes, toiletries and talk. Several people had hands and feet wrapped in gauze and bandages.

One fellow told me his thumb had been severed while he was riding a train from Guatemala. He had been traveling for a month and walking in the desert for four days. Three young women wrapped in colorful ponchos asked if we had warm jackets. Their hair hung to their waist in long thick braids.

—————

I see a little boy and a group of young men, all from Honduras. They have been walking or riding on a train for twenty-one days. The child is nine years old, and his father tells me, speaking in perfect English, that he is happy to be here and has no intention of trying to cross into the United States. To my amazement, the father has a Brooklyn accent.

His history is this: He lived in Brooklyn for ten years, was deported in 2004 and returned to Honduras. I asked the father why he has taken his young son and made this long and dangerous journey to the U.S.-Mexican border.

"Honduras is full of soldiers with guns everywhere. There are no jobs and I am a skilled automotive repairman. I do body work. I do not want my son to grow up where he is not safe going to school because of the violence. And then there are the drugs."

"So what are your plans?" I ask.

He says he will find work repairing cars in Nogales, Mexico, and eventually open his own shop. He acquired his skills in New York and believes he can do well in Nogales. The man is positive, upbeat and eager to put his dreams into action.

"Gringos will bring their cars to me from the U.S. because I am good, I am honest and I'll give them a good price."

You can smell hope on this guy.

His son, Kevin, is holding a bundle of clothes and a blanket from the *comedor*. Looking tired, he gives me a grin. When I took a photo of father and son, several other men from Honduras crowded into the picture. They were together, and I got the sense that these folks were going to make it.

One fellow held up two fingers, giving me the peace sign. There was more hope here than despair. It felt good to be in this crowd today.

—⁓—

Our visitors from Wisconsin and Idaho were overwhelmed by the happy confusion and activity. They pitched in and helped sort the bags of clothes, shyly and tentatively passing out the shoes and toiletries and making connections with the pilgrims.

On the long walk back to the U.S. border and my warm, safe life in Arizona, I wondered what it would take for me to travel thousands of miles on trains, on foot, with no money or credit cards or a waiting family. And what if I had a child with me?

I tried to wrap my brain around this thought. It was impossible for me to play this scene out in my mind. And yet I had spent the last several hours with people who had taken that very risk.

As we approached the border, I saw the street peddler with the fever and gave him a handful of aspirin. He gave me a weary grin, and we continued on our way.

CHAPTER SIX

Life Lessons

One morning I was driving to town with my husband and we spotted two young men with backpacks racing across the road in front of us, running along the railroad tracks. Wryly commenting, "Well, ya' think they're joggers?" my husband once again pointed out to me the baffling dissonance of living the reality of the borderlands.

At times it just hits me in the face. I watched as the two young men, dressed in jeans and hoodies and carrying jugs of water, sped into the desert, disappearing into thickets of mesquite trees. Possibly I had talked with these men at the *comedor* earlier in the week. Maybe they were wearing the clothes and shoes the Samaritans had provided.

Silently I hoped they would make it to their destination safely. Maybe they will become successful entrepreneurs and earn a million dollars. Maybe they will open a terrific chain of Mexican restaurants. I want them to begin building their American dream, or at least have the ability to cross back and forth into Mexico with visas and work permits.

Thumbs up

I said a silent prayer for their safety. I'm on their side. I don't want them to hide anymore.

Rationally I know that these fellows are most likely undocumented Mexican migrants breaking the law, crossing our borders without the necessary legal entry papers. I respect law and order and the stability it brings to my life in the United States. When people cross our borders, the country needs to have an orderly process in place.

I want these young men, who looked like they were running for their lives, to have the chance to work and earn an honest day's wage—to begin a life where they can support themselves and their families. Morally I cannot accept that we treat people who simply want to work as if they were dangerous criminals. I want my rational, emotional and spiritual sensibilities to be congruent. I'm tired of the ambiguity and the gray areas of life on the border. I'm tired of people telling me that migrants are breaking the law and need to be stopped. I want clarity.

It has been a year since I began volunteering with the Samaritans at the *comedor*. I am continually astounded that the migrants open up to us in such a profound way, given the abundance of negative sentiment toward Latinos in the United States. Talking about their experiences comes easily to the men; the women are more reserved and rarely make eye contact. But their body language says a lot: Eyes are cast down, they are slumped over at the breakfast tables and they rarely smile. Their bodies are contracted inward, as if their torsos were a little cave in which to hide and be safe.

The children, however, bring life to the *comedor*. Everybody perks up when there are children around. A couple of cats live in the shelter and the children pet them and feed them scraps from the table. Kids act like kids when there are animals to be petted and loved.

Children cannot help where they are born, and yet our country punishes people for what they cannot help being. We are either born here or we are born across some arbitrary border.

I think about that simple fact. How come the hundreds of people I have met this past year work harder, speak intelligently and fluently in several languages and exhibit a strength and wisdom seldom seen this side of the border? How come they will most likely live a life of poverty and drudgery and I will be surrounded with the comforts and safety of my home?

At the *comedor* I've seen children who have been separated from their parents The babies and toddlers do not smile. They don't cry either. Looking off into space, the children are trying to remove themselves from the trauma they have experienced. These kids wear the most serious expressions I have ever seen. The faces look like the dolls in department-store windows at Christmas—passive, vacant, unblinking. Petting the cats that hang around the *comedor* will bring a smile to a child's face, though. Bless the animals.

I have witnessed young men breaking down in tears when asked how they are doing. Others are mute, unable to respond to any interaction; they instead isolate themselves in a corner. Sometimes they rock back and forth in despair. They mechanically move their forks back and forth as they eat the breakfast, but their eyes are a million miles away. They walk stiffly, rigidly, as if there is a paralysis of the soul. It is humbling to witness people at such a low point in their lives, and often I look away, feeling numb.

~~~

One gentleman from Guatemala, César, speaks with me about his journey north. Another migrant helps me translate exactly what César is saying. He has a missing tooth, and his thin angular frame bears scars and welts. Beaten and tortured in his homeland, he tells me his entire family was murdered in the past year.

He is seeking asylum in the United States. It has taken him eight days to get here, hopping trains and walking.

"It is too dangerous for me to stay in Guatemala. I have the scars from my enemies. There are drugs and killings. I cannot go back."

César stops for a moment and looks into my eyes. "Besides, when your family is killed, you have no place to cry."

I sit in stunned silence and listen to César's story. César slowly eats his breakfast of scrambled eggs and beans, staring off into space. There doesn't appear to be an ounce of fat on his gaunt body.

—␣␣—

The Samaritans direct this gentleman to the U.S. Consulate, hoping his story will reach the right ears, a humane advocate for César. According to the Executive Office of Immigration Review, only 2 percent of Mexicans seeking asylum in this country actually obtain it. For Guatemalans, 4.5 percent seeking asylum in 2009 were allowed to enter this country; 3,458 had applied.[19] This does not bode well for César.

Nevertheless, César is animated and hopeful in his conversations with me. He is not beaten down as he gratefully finishes his breakfast. I get the feeling that things can only get better for César. How could things get any worse after losing his entire family?

César and I sit together and speak of the future. His face has the look of intelligence. I watch him gather up a newspaper and read a few articles. He stands out in his bright red T-shirt, speaking a mix of Spanish and English. Picking up a warm jacket and some jeans, he leaves the *comedor* and begins walking toward the U.S. Consulate. His story stays with me for months.

I never see him again.

WOMEN ON THE MOVE

The women usually stay together. They sit with their children and babies at the long tables and are silent. Many bonded with each other while crossing the desert, especially if they were abandoned by their *coyote* guides.

Some met while locked up in a detention center, and they are now cemented in a friendship that involves life-or-death experiences. The women rarely talk about what has happened. The sisters tell me that 80 percent or more have been assaulted, raped and beaten. Some are impregnated by *coyote* guides during their journey in the desert. Like the children, they rarely smile, and they have a look of profound sadness and shame.

I ache to talk to them but am held back because of the language barrier. They are reserved and not as willing to share their experiences as the men. I respect their silence and often just put my hand on their shoulders in a sort of silent solidarity.

―――

A Samaritan colleague fluent in Spanish speaks with three women who have been in the desert for eight days. They tell us they are heading to New York City, where their husbands wait for them. After four days in the desert, their *coyote* guide abandoned them because they could not keep up with the group. One of the women appears to be mentally challenged. They were lost for four days and took refuge in an *arroyo* in the desert, living on a chocolate bar and a small amount of water.

Miraculously, Border Patrol agents rescued them and took them to a detention center. Denied food and water for twenty-four hours in the prison, the starving, dehydrated women were finally given food. The plates of food were thrown at these women, and the guard told them, "You're nothing but dogs, so eat off the floor."

Bearing witness to this abuse is horrifying. I believe every word of their story. The mentally challenged young woman looks to be twenty years old. She wanders around the *comedor* smiling at everyone in a sort of trance.

"I love all the beautiful smiles," she tells everyone she sees.

She is in another world.

And what about the plans for this tragic group of women? They are still determined to cross again and try to get to New York. It is an inexplicable moment for all of us who listen to their story. They cannot be dissuaded. It is as if they do not care if they die during the journey. Our warnings and talk of death in the desert pass right over their heads and out the door.

I cannot get these women out of my mind.

—⁓—

Undocumented immigrants live in constant fear of

deportation. Any chance encounter with U.S. immigration officials can leave an undocumented person behind bars and in deportation proceedings.

The impact that deportations have on families and communities in the United States is less obvious. Entire immigrant neighborhoods in American towns and cities live in fear that their financial stability will unravel if a parent is picked up and they will lose their children. Individuals can be locked up for months or years. Many Mexican American neighborhoods in the United States have mobilized with a secret network of caretakers who step in if a child comes home from school and his parents are missing.

I met a woman at the *comedor* who was born in Puebla, Mexico, and brought to the United States when she was six weeks old. She has lived in Phoenix for twenty-seven years. Married to an American, she has three children and was the manager of a well-known fast-food drive-in.

This woman graduated from an American high school and attended a community college here. Like many Latinos, she didn't seek citizenship or legal residency because life got in the way. She married, had children and didn't think anyone would go to the trouble to check up on a law-abiding person. She speaks English fluently and knows very few Spanish words. Since her birth and subsequent migration to the United States, she had never been back to Mexico.

Her name is Rosa, and she was picked up in Phoenix for allegedly cruising through a red light. Rosa denies this allegation.

"I noticed a sheriff's car following me for two miles, so I followed the speed limit and paid attention to all the traffic

signs," she tells me. "I'm not stupid. I saw I was being followed by the police car. I didn't break any laws."

When the sheriff turned on his rotating lights, Rosa had
a moment of trepidation. She had no criminal record, not
even a speeding ticket. The officer asked her immediately if
she was a legal citizen. Instead of answering his question,
Rosa asked the officer why he was stopping her. Again she
was asked about her legal status. She replied that she did
not have to answer that question.

At this point the officer asked for her driver's license and
registration. She produced both. Running the license
through the system, the sheriff ascertained that Rosa was not
a documented citizen of the United States. Though she had
been brought here when she was an infant of six weeks, she
did not have the papers and documentation of citizenship.

Because she believed she was not breaking any traffic
laws, she told the officer he was racially profiling and he had
no right to stop her. This did not help matters.

Rosa was immediately taken to Eloy, Arizona, where
there is a detention center. Of course, she was terrified and
hysterical about her three children, who had no idea what
was happening to their mother.

Her lawyer in Eloy told her that a hearing would take
three or four months to begin and she would probably be
deported anyway. After several days, she signed deportation papers just to get out of the prison and was transferred
to Nogales, where she sought refuge at the *comedor.* Sign-
ing these papers barred her from reentering the United
States for at least ten years, a fact she did not understand at
the time.

When I meet Rosa at the *comedor*, she is barely able to keep her composure. The sisters are providing her with shelter at *Casa Nazaret*, and Rosa helps me fold clothes and pass them out to the migrants. The work is keeping her sane in her topsy-turvy world.

The Samaritans and the sisters provide Internet access for Rosa, a cell phone for calls to her children and books to read. She loves Tom Clancy thrillers and the Harry Potter series, and we give her these books and some popular music CDs. She helps out daily at the *comedor* and, of course, loves talking to Americans about TV shows, her job in Phoenix and her kids.

Rosa is now divorced from her husband and he has not taken responsibility or interest in caring for the children. She has a brother living in Chicago, and he has temporary custody of her family. The children are enrolled in a Chicago school, and Rosa frequently communicates with them by phone and e-mail.

Before 1996, deportation was a small enterprise and judges often exercised compassion for people who had no history of dangerous criminal activity. Then came September 11, 2001, and border security changed dramatically. The tragedy of the World Trade Center and the deaths of over three thousand people put this country on hyper-alert.

The border became the focus of attention, and armed guards patrolled the ports of entry as if there were a declared war twenty feet from the line. But there have been no alleged Muslim terrorists detained at the U.S.-Mexican border. None.

Drug runners? Yes—mostly transported through ports of entry in cars and trucks. Illicit substances pass through the phalanx of federal agents, drug-sniffing dogs, X-ray machines and Border Patrol officers. The hunger for recreational highs knows no bounds in the United States.

After two months of reflection and counseling at the *comedor* and *Casa Nazaret*, Rosa decided to move to Obregón, Mexico, where she was offered a job with minimal pay. I think about Rosa, with her children in Chicago and her future a shambles because she was followed one day by a police officer on her way home from work in Phoenix.

Rosa was a perfect candidate for the DREAMers program, the series of measures proclaimed by President Obama which took effect on August 15, 2012. She was under 31 years of age, was brought to this country at six weeks of age, was a high school graduate and had no criminal history. Rosa's future is in limbo because she was randomly picked up by the police less that two weeks before she could apply for deferred action.

BIG ISSUES, SMALL ACTS

Volunteering at the *comedor* swallows me up. The issues are enormous. Thousands of people pass through this place, all of them desperate to create a better life. I cannot fix the enormous pain I see in their faces. A different culture and language separate us. Our life experiences are so different. And yet, there is a connection here.

Many of the people I meet each week are migrating for economic and social reasons. They want to work. They do not want to live in fear. A guest-worker program allowing immigrants to come into the U.S. for a period of time to seek employment and small business privileges seems like a good thing. Making a living wage in Mexico seems like an even better thing. My migrant friends yearn for their homes, their birthplace, their extended families. They would gladly stay in Mexico if they could earn a living wage.

In the past, guest workers in the United States were not always treated like guests. Rather, many were exploited and abused, and their visas tied them to only one employer. If they were unhappy with their employer, they couldn't leave or change jobs. It was not much different from serfdom.

Many workers were routinely cheated out of wages, forced to live in squalid conditions and held virtually captive by employers who seized their documents. If they complained, they were threatened with deportation.

The United States needs seasonal workers in the fields, in the seafood industry, in construction, in the service industries and in a multitude of infrastructure projects. The agricultural industry depends on immigrant labor to plant and harvest the food we eat. The bridges need repair, the highways are full of cracks and many schools have not been maintained.

The restaurant industry depends on immigrants to keep the businesses running smoothly. They wash the dishes, clean the floors and become skilled chefs in the kitchens of our cities. Yet there are twice-weekly deportation flights from JFK Airport in New York City to Puebla, Mexico, filled with migrant workers without the proper papers.

I met a man who owns three restaurants in New York City. He tells me that the restaurant industry would disappear without the hiring of undocumented immigrants.

"When a person has a Green Card, he demands more in wages than a restaurant can afford." He tells me that hiring the undocumented is the only way to get the dishes washed, the vegetables chopped. He cannot afford to hire people with a Green Card.

Working in the kitchens of New York restaurants is a first step for many undocumented migrants who are looking for economic survival. The restaurant employer pays these workers slightly more than minimum wage. It is a beginning for many restaurant workers.

The man with the three restaurants has personally sponsored immigrants who wish to apply for citizenship. He spoke in practical terms about the need for temporary guest-worker visas so migrants are not living in fear, threatened with deportation.

Most Americans refuse to do this work. The belief that migrant workers are taking away jobs from Americans is unfounded.

Increased immigration would boost the U.S. economy. According to David Brooks, politically conservative columnist for *The New York Times,* immigrants are 30 percent more likely to start businesses than native-born Americans.[20]

Immigrants with low-skilled jobs contribute to the lower cost of food as well as affordable housekeeping and child care. Living standards rise and more women are able to work outside the home. In the neighborhoods of Los Angeles, entire streets are taken over by Latino landscape workers and nannies. While the Anglos are at work, the Latinos are caring for the upscale homes and gardens. Children play in nearby parks, with their Spanish-speaking nannies keeping them safe from harm.

New immigrants may start out as landscape workers, domestic help, food-service employees and construction workers, but by the second and third generations, the job profiles resemble those of the native-born. The undocumented worker is less likely to wind up in prison or in mental hospitals than U.S. citizens.[21]

I have met migrant gourmet chefs, automotive repairmen, skilled seamstresses and computer-savvy teenagers. Many want to work in the United States for only short periods and then return to their homes in Latin America. Others want to return to their families in the United States and be free to cross back and forth into Mexico to visit relatives and friends on special occasions.

I spend a lot of time reading about numbers—the numbers of deportations, the numbers of deaths in the desert, the numbers of killings by drug cartels, the millions of dollars spent building detention centers and walls.

These numbers are people.

The issue of illegal immigration has been left to fester for decades. Calls for greater border security and a bigger, higher wall are part of the angry obstructionism that permeates the political climate. Both Democrats and Republicans balk at tackling the issue. The topic arouses intense emotions, and the battle to pass comprehensive immigration reform may end up making the political struggle over health-care legislation look like a walk in the park.

My work in the borderlands is about compassion and service.

Instead of focusing on drugs, trafficking and terrorism, I want a borderlands where we concentrate on commerce, tourism, families, bicultural events, great restaurants,

music and all the arts of Latin America. But on a deeper
level, I have learned that the real work on the border is
about giving love, no matter what.

I want the faith community to challenge federal policy
on immigration and become a change agent instead of a
passive observer of unjust laws. The language of faith seems
out of place in the halls of power and money, but the church
must speak out when the least of us are dying each day in
the deserts of Arizona.

The United States will have a Mexican-American future.
This scares people. I want this cultural shift to be a positive
thing where there is a welcome mat at the border. The best
way to confront the issue of eleven million undocumented
people in the United States who have violated our anti-
quated immigration laws is to fix the laws. A more humane
way to confront the issue of the migration of thousands of
Latinos is to offer safe passage and a beginning level of
work.

WAY PAST TIME

Sometimes I sit at the *comedor* watching the migrating travelers in their ragged jeans and worn-out shoes and think
about a world without poverty. Or at least a borderlands
where we've eliminated this level of impoverishment.

The barriers we have erected to keep out migrant movement are antithetical to the basic human right of self-deter-
mination. The people I am watching today want to work
hard, support their families and live without fear of violence and corruption.

The gargantuan wall that separates my country from Mexico is an abomination. It says that you are brown, I am white, and I don't want you here. We may speak of developing our economic ties and trade agreements with Latin America, but as long as we are building a wall to secure our borders, we are speaking with a forked tongue.

We welcome the tomatoes and chilies and papayas from Mexico because there is money to be made. But we are locking out the people. You can die in our deserts trying to get here, and we will look the other way. Keep the truckloads of tomatoes coming, however. And while you're at it, keep the prices down.

The humanitarian costs are huge. Thousands have died in the Sonoran Desert. Millions who are living in the United States fear deportation and separation from their children and families.

Fifty years from now our children and grandchildren will ask us why we did not do something. Why did our government not recognize the tragedy of an immigration policy of exclusion? Why did the government contribute to this atrocity?

Maybe, just maybe, the lifting of immigration barriers will result in unimaginable gains measured in trillions of dollars. A large percentage of people have gone from abject poverty to financial stability by moving across borders. This is the story of most of our ancestors who crossed the pond seeking a better life. So why don't we just let people move wherever they want to go?

We lose a lot of money by not maximizing human potential. I see artists, skilled auto mechanics, chefs and displaced farmers every Tuesday I spend in Nogales. According to the research of Michael Clemens, a noted economics scholar, decades' worth of immigrants have had minimal impact on the American wage-earner. In fact, immigrants have reduced the average wage in this country by fractions of a percent, if at all[22].

Challenging the notion that immigrants take away American jobs, Clemens has examined the agricultural job market. For every three seasonal workers brought into the United States, one new job is created—that of the manager, which is usually an American. Also, workers buy things, which means a market for producing and selling those things. So for every busload of sixty Mexican farmworkers, there are twenty additional jobs waiting to be filled, most likely by American farmers.[23]

The United States has championed an "enforcement first" approach to immigration management for two and a half decades—an approach that has yet to work. We are attempting to implement unworkable laws that in fact facilitate unauthorized immigration. Undocumented workers who are already in the United States are locked in. They cannot travel freely back and forth to Mexico for weddings, funerals, family events. So they stay, living in fear, praying that they will not be discovered.

Latinos who are locked out of our country risk their lives to cross our borders trying to reunite with families, escape violence in their own villages or find economic stability. If you are a Latino without papers, you are either locked in or locked out.

Our philosophy of "enforcement first" has become the nation's singular response to the undocumented. Congressional discussions center almost entirely on building enforcement programs—higher walls, more boots on the ground.

The enforcement-only approach has consistently failed to work for twenty-seven years. It is a narrow view of a much broader issue. True immigration reform must include a pathway to legal status for the undocumented people who are already living in this country—eleven million of them.

In spite of the wall and the weaponry, millions have made it through the barriers and live in the United States. Legislation must include flexible avenues for future immigration. The system is broken. Continuing to push for more border security and an increased Border Patrol presence is a fool's errand. If we create an orderly legal process whereby we allow people to pass back and forth across our borders, we will need fewer Border Patrol agents, not more.[24]

Today's immigrants have some advantages that previous waves of migrants did not; our national culture is more accepting of diversity, especially among the young people. There are new obstacles, however. Earlier immigrants, including my own ancestors, were not breaking the law by living in the United States. Today's undocumented pilgrims are.

Probably every Latino family living as citizens of the United States knows of at least one person, quite possibly a family member, who is living here without legal documentation—the proper papers. An undocumented status brings many disadvantages that inhibit moving ahead financially and socially.

Unauthorized parents are less willing to ask for a raise or change of position that might help them climb the economic ladder. They are hesitant to become involved in their children's school, to call the police if there is trouble and to start their own business. The risks are too high. They are living in a shadow world. We are losing their creativity and their strong work ethic.

There are millions of men, women and children living under the radar in fear. It is time to bring them in from the dark.

SWEET MEMORIES

I remember frequent trips to Nogales, Mexico, with my family and visiting relatives from Iowa and Minnesota when I was a kid growing up in Tucson. My mother proudly marched everyone across the border through a ramshackle gate often dangling on one hinge. This was the U.S. entrance into Mexico. The rest of the boundary line was a haphazard barbed-wire fence, usually two drooping strands, which as kids we could crawl under if the line by the gate was too long. When you reached the edge of Nogales, there was no fence at all. Nogales was one big city with a meandering line of fence trailing up and down the hills. It was difficult to tell if you were in the United States or Mexico.

There were a few U.S. Customs agents milling around, mostly opening the gate politely and greeting everyone with smiles. The Mexican Customs agents welcomed the tourists and, more often than not, were invisible. None of our family traveled abroad, so we did not own a passport. As a child, I carried no identification.

We'd spend the day strolling the venues and shops of

Avenida Obregón, shopping for hand-tooled leather purses and cowboy hats for our Midwestern relatives. Lunch was at Elvira's, where free shots of tequila were offered on a silver tray. The whole experience was exotic and festive. The Iowa relatives still talk about it fifty years later.

My mother had her favorite booths that she visited, and the proprietors could see her coming blocks away. They knew that money would be spent, and there was a convivial give-and-take as my mother bartered with the shopkeepers.

Always we stopped for photos on a street corner where a photographer waited with his burro and a cart. I still have pictures from those hot afternoons in Nogales with the aunts and uncles and the big sombrero.

As a teenager and young adult, I was a frequent visitor to Nogales and loved to attend the bullfights. Political correctness was not a part of my DNA during those years. I loved the pageantry of the bullring, the color of the costumes, the music of the band, which was usually out of tune and a bit tipsy, the warm beer in paper cups and the ballet of life and death danced by the *banderilleros*, the *picadors* and the *matador*. Sometimes the bull was spared if the fight was valiant, allowing him to return to his home pasture to live out his life. More often the matador killed the bull. The crowd cheered wildly no matter who fell in a pool of blood. It was primal, it was drama, it was Mexico.

Afterward there was dinner and revelry at the Mexican *cantinas*. The crowds of Mexican nationals and visiting Americans on those Sunday trips to Nogales were a global connection that was possible just a short drive from my Tucson home. I thought I was the luckiest young woman alive to have both worlds at my doorstep.

I know I cannot go back to those innocent times, but I remember well the camaraderie and friendship I felt with our neighbors to the south. We would sing the old Mexican ballads together far into the night.

I want a piece of that feeling of friendship with Mexico for my children and grandchildren. I want my children to experience the things I love about the Latino culture: the music, the art, the food, the ability to live in joy and celebration, the traditions and the generosity of spirit.

I miss the rickety fence and the dangling gate. I want a welcome mat on our side of the fence.

Special Thanks

The people who do the frontline work on the border are a special breed. An ability to keep your heart open to both suffering and the good times is essential. These people have been my mentors and role models.

Father Sean Carroll, S.J. and the Kino Border Initiative are on the frontlines every day providing food, counsel and love to thousands of the most vulnerable people in this hemisphere. KBI relies on donations to provide direct humanitarian relief services to migrants. The address for KBI is: Kino Border Initiative, P.O. Box 159, Nogales, AZ 85628-0159. Its Web site is: www.kinoborderinitiative.org.

The Sisters of the Eucharist are love in action. They never stop moving or caring. I am especially indebted to Sisters Lorena, Rosalba and Alma for their tireless service and their salsa music.

Shura Wallin is the founder and prime mover of the Green Valley Samaritans. Shura's ability to serve the forgotten people stranded on our border with humor and compassion is worthy of a hundred gold stars. The walk to the *comedor* is always an adventure with Shura (if you can keep up with her). The Green Valley Samaritans accept donations to further the work in the desert and at the *comedor*. The Web site is: www.gvsamaritans.org. Donations can be sent to: Good Shepherd United Church of Christ, 17750 S. La Canada Drive, Sahuarita, AZ 85629.

The Border Community Alliance (BCA) is an innovative and exciting nonprofit organization to be reckoned with in southern Arizona. In collaboration with its Mexican partner, *Fundación del Empresariado Sonorense* (FESAC), the two organizations work together to improve the quality of life for border communities. Bob Phillips, Bill Neubauer, M.D., and Alma Cota de Yanez have inspired me with their vision about economic, humanitarian and cultural issues in the borderlands. I am honored to be a board member and watch with amazement as the two organizations evolve and go where angels fear to tread. The website is: www.bordercommunityalliance.com

Ricardo Osburn is a commercial airline pilot who speaks Spanish fluently and easily engages the migrants in conversation. He spent years as a pilot flying to Guatemala and loves to practice his Spanish while swapping stories with the travelers.

Harry Smith is a retired firefighter from New York who lives in Green Valley, Arizona. He has organized his church to donate heavy blankets during the winter months. Harry can be seen carrying several gallons of water to remote stations in the Arizona desert on the hottest days of the year.

Mike Casey has expertise in desert searches. He organizes teams of searchers and coordinates the efforts to find lost and injured migrants in the desert. He makes sure the Samaritan van is loaded with food, water, medical supplies and clothing for those who might need help. Mike has spent time in Ethiopia and other exotic far-off places building schools and clinics.

Jack McGarvey has a history with the Samaritans, and for many years transported bags of supplies in his van across the border to the *comedor*. He is also a skilled writer and contributes cogent editorials to local newspapers and journals.

I value the advice, direction and insights I get each day from Samaritans Sharon Chamberlin, Bette Mulley, Jaime Brusstar, Ricardo Calabro and the "two Johns."

Ruby Firecat, my neighbor and mentor in all things border-related, has plied me with desert wisdom and her excellent tequila these past years.

John Toso, photographer and nomadic pilgrim, was brave enough to accompany me on a trip to the *comedor*, to the dentist in Nogales and on a desert search. And he always answers my e-mails promptly with a humorous twinkle.

Jerry and Bette Ervin have supplied the Samaritans with carloads of clothes and shared their editing expertise while I was writing this book. Growing up together as teenagers, Jerry and I have prowled the desert and remember when Tucson was a small city surrounded by few houses and lots of saguaro cacti.

Linda Eckhardt has been in my corner for decades. Her writing skills inspire and captivate, as does her blog, "Everybody Eats News" (www.everybodyeatsnews.com).

Bill Broyles, author and desert wanderer, told me to write

a book years ago. I brushed off the idea for a long time but am so happy to have him as a guide on this path. We also sang in a church choir when we were teens, and I treasure this shared history.

Bruce Dinges, writer and editor of the *Arizona Historical Review*, has been a cheerleader and adviser in my efforts to make sense of border issues.

Cheyenne and Sage, our two kids, encouraged me to write a blog when I wasn't sure what a blog was. Their lives give me the juice to keep going.

Lester Weil, *mi esposo*, has been my quiet, steadfast rock, supporting me with his love and patience in spite of it all.

Photos are by John Toso, Martin Ethington and Peg Bowden.

Peg Bowden writes a blog about her experiences at *el comedor* and on the border. The postings can be accessed at www.arroya.org.

Endnotes

1 Immigration papers are given to migrants when they are deported from the United States into Mexico. Migrants are taken to an immigration office known as *Repatriación Humana del Instituto Nacional de Migración* (Human Repatriation of the National Migration Institute), in Nogales, Mexico. All deportees must have these papers before being served at the *comedor*. In this way the aid workers can screen who are migrants and who are not.

2 Leonard Cohen, "Sisters of Mercy," *Songs of Leonard Cohen*, 2007, audio CD

3 "Vista Father of Five Dies in Arizona Desert After Being Deported," Edward Sifuentes, *North County Times*, May 26, 2012

4 "Numb to Carnage, Mexicans Find Diversions, and Life Goes On," Randal C. Archibold and Damien Cave, *The New York Times*, May 15, 2012

5 "Deportations From Arizona Are Down Sharply," Perla Treviso, *Arizona Daily Star*, Jan. 26, 2013

6 "Throwing Good Money After Bad: Immigration Enforcement," *Immigration Policy Center*, May 26, 2010. President Obama increased this budget by $600 million in a special supplemental package for even more border security.

7 "U.S. Border Security: Huge Costs with Mixed Results," Martha Mendoza, AZCentral.com, June 22, 2011. The length of the U.S./Mexico border is 1,969 miles; the length of the border fence is 650 miles.

8 "Operation Streamline, SB1070, CCA, Immigration and Private Prisons, and How It All Connects," *Tucson Citizen*, Oct. 21, 2010

9 "NAFTA and U.S. Corn Subsidies: Explaining the Displacement of Mexico's Corn Farms," R. Relinger, *Prospect Journal of International Affairs at UCSD*, 2010. The World Bank reports that in 2001, 6.2 million tons of U.S. corn were sent to Mexico.

In 2010, the U.S. corn exports grew to 21 times their pre-NAFTA level. Many Mexican farmers were left with two options: stay on the family farm and starve or go north. Most were forced to seek work in the United States. This was a devastating blow to family farms. Nearly 1.4 million Mexican farms went bankrupt by 2008, resulting in 600,000 Mexicans migrating north to the United States.

10 "Let a Thousand Corn Stalks Bloom," Kent Paterson, *The Progressive Populist,* Sept. 1, 2007. NAFTA has not been a boon to the working class of the U.S., as 750,000 jobs have been outsourced to Mexico. Large U.S. corporations like Monsanto and DuPont have moved across the border. The soil, which has served Mexico for generations, will soon be sterile and dead.

11 "Will Monsanto Destroy Mexico's Corn?" Charlotte Silver, *Al Jazeera,* Dec. 14, 2012

12 "How Much Petroleum Does the United States Import and From Where," *U.S. Energy Information Administration,* June 3, 2013

13 *"Cielito Lindo,"* Quirino Mendoza y Cortéz, 1882

14 *"Dios Está Aqui,"* Raul Galeano, composer, born in Buenos Aires, Argentina, now living in Florida.

15 "State of Arizona Immigration Detention Centers," July 7, 2011, http://www.immigrationequality.org/2011/07/the-state-of-arizona-immigration-detention-centers/

16 "In Their Own Words," *Arizona ACLU Report,* 2011, www.acluaz.org/detention-report-2011

17 PBS documentary, Oct. 18, 2011, http://www.pbs.org/wgbh/pages/frontline/lost-in-detention/

18 "The Great Divide," Charles M. Sennott, *Global Post,* January 16, 2013, www.globalpost.com

19 *Guatemala Human Rights Commission,* 2009, www.ghrc-usa.org

20 "The Easy Problem," David Brooks, *The New York Times,* Jan. 31, 2013

21 "The Economics of Immigration Reform," Michael Greenstone and Adam Looney, the Hamilton Project, *UpFront,* January 29, 2013

22 "Economics and Emigration: Trillion-dollar Bills on the Sidewalk?" Michael A. Clemens, *Journal of Economic Perspectives,* Vol. 25, Number 3, Summer 2011

23 Ibid.

24 "The Fallacy of Enforcement First," *Immigration Policy Center,* May 9, 2013, http://www.immigrationpolicy.org/just-facts/fallacy-enforcement-first

Spanish Glossary

agave: a succulent desert plant with rosettes of narrow spiny leaves and tall flower spikes, common in the Southwestern U.S. and Mexico.

banderillero: a matador's assistant in a bullfight who thrusts a barbed spear into the neck and shoulders of the bull.

cantina: a small bar or luncheon cafe.

Casa Nazaret: the House of Nazareth, a shelter operated by the Sisters of the Eucharist in Nogales, Sonora. The shelter is a place of safety for women and children.

chile verde: a spicy stew of green *chiles*, pork, and vegetables.

comedor: a dining area. The popular name of the aid station for migrant travelers in Nogales, Sonora, Mexico.

farmacia: a pharmacy.

gringo: slang for a white American or European.

javelina: a wild peccary that roams in small herds in the Sonoran Desert.

Los Estados Unidos: The United States.

matador: a bullfighter.

maquiladora: a factory in Mexico run by a foreign company. Many are located along the U.S./Mexico border.

menudo: a spicy Mexican soup made with tripe, *chile* peppers, onion, hominy, and spices. A traditional remedy for a hangover.

ocotillo: a spiny, scarlet-flowered desert plant of the southwestern U.S. and Mexico.

picador: a bullfighter on horseback who pricks the bull with a lance in the neck in order to weaken the animal and goad it.

ramada: an open shelter roofed with branches or brush designed to provide shade.

salsa: a spicy sauce made with tomatoes, onions and *chile* peppers used as a condiment in Mexican cuisine.

taquería: a small outdoor venue that serves tacos and other Mexican street food.

Virgen de Guadalupe: a celebrated Catholic image in Mexico of the Virgin Mary.

Acronyms and Border Organizations

BCA: Border Community Alliance, a nonprofit organization that identifies current and emerging issues unique to the borderlands. The mission is to support the educational, cultural, social, healthcare, and economic development of the U.S./Mexico border region. A binational partner of FESAC, in Nogales, Sonora.

CCA: Corrections Corporation of America, the private corporation that owns and operates detention centers where undocumented people are incarcerated in the United States.

DREAM: Development, Relief and Education for Alien Minors, an American legislative proposal that would provide conditional permanent residency to children who arrived in the U.S. as minors. The bill would hasten the path toward citizenship. As of March, 2014, the bill is still being debated in Congress.

FESAC: *Fundación del Empresariado Sonorense,* a nonprofit organization in Nogales, Sonora, serving the people of Nogales. Also a binational partner of the Border Community Alliance.

Green Card: a type of visa whereby people from other countries may live, work and study in the U.S. Some 50,000 Green Cards are issued each year.

ICE: Immigration and Customs Enforcement, a department within the U.S. Department of Homeland Security.

KBI: Kino Border Initiative, a binational organization that works in the area of migration in Nogales, Sonora, Mexico and Nogales, Arizona. The mission is to promote immigration policies that affirm the dignity of all people.

Migrant Trail Walk: an annual 75 mile walk along a known migrant trail from Sasabe, Sonora, Mexico to Tucson, Arizona. The walk is sponsored by several organizations interested in raising awareness of the immigration experience of thousands of undocumented pilgrims in the United States.

NAFTA: North American Free Trade Agreement, a regulation implemented on Jan. 1, 1994, that eventually eliminated tariffs in order to increase economic activity between the U.S., Mexico and Canada. The results have been controversial. Millions of Mexican farmers have been forced from their land in Central and Southern Mexico due to the lowered, subsidized imports of corn and other agricultural products from the U.S.

NMD: No More Deaths, a nonprofit organization in Arizona whose mission is to end death and suffering on the U.S./Mexico border through civil action.

Samaritans: The Green Valley/Sahuarita Samaritans is a nonprofit organization whose mission is to prevent deaths in the desert. Members go on desert searches looking for lost or injured migrants, volunteer at *el comedor* in Mexico, and participate in water drops, delivering life-saving water.

PEG BOWDEN is a retired public health nurse living on a ranch in the San Cayetano Mountains of southern Arizona. For thirty years she practiced nursing in Oregon, but she is basically a desert rat. She returned to the Sonoran Desert to paint, practice the piano, and pound on the timpani in a local concert band. The politics of the borderlands brought out a passion to record what she was seeing. Peg writes a blog about the experience of the migrant called *La Frontera: the border,* which can be accessed at www.arroya.org

She lives with her husband, Lester Weil, two dogs, a cat, and a lot of open range cattle.

CPSIA information can be obtained
at www.ICGtesting.com
Printed in the USA
BVHW070927061019
560141BV00005B/40/P